DEDICATION

To my granddaughter
Bentley Reese Nowery

ACKNOWLEDGMENT

I would like to thank Andy Stimer
for his friendship and partnership
in writing with me, believing in me
and encouraging me
to live a life of adventurous faith.

CONTENTS

FOREWORD
by Dr. John C. Maxwell 7

INTRODUCTION 11

Chapter 1
CARPE DIEM
Stewarding Every Day...19

Chapter 2
RAPID RESPONSE
Stewarding Every Opportunity 33

Chapter 3
INFLUENCE & IMPACT
Stewarding Every Relationship 55

Chapter 4
PRAYING WITH PURPOSE
Stewarding Every Concern 79

Chapter 5
WHAT'S IN YOUR HAND?
Stewarding Every Ability 93

Chapter 6
MORE THAN MONEY
Stewarding Every Asset 113

Chapter 7
KEEPING THE FAITH
Stewarding Every Commitment 131

REFERENCES 157

FOREWORD

~ ~ ~

By John C. Maxwell

This is a compelling book.

When Kirk Nowery told me he had been inspired to write *360° Stewardship* after reading my own book, *The 360° Leader*, I encouraged him to go for it. I was confident that the result would be undeniably instructive and unforgettably inspirational—and I was right! *360° Stewardship* is a book to be read more than once. It is *that* valuable. You will be challenged to think about things of great importance in these seven extraordinary chapters, and you will be captured by the significance of stewardship as never before.

360° Stewardship addresses seven essential elements of a life wisely lived. Let me give you a preview of each one...

Stewarding Every Day. Few of us speak Latin, but we know the meaning of *Carpe Diem*—"seize the day." God allots to each of us the same 24 hours in each day, and we must steward those hours with wisdom. This introductory chapter tackles that challenge and provides a practical but very personal guide to seizing each day for God's glory.

Stewarding Every Opportunity. We are blessed with so many opportunities in life, and to be effective stewards we must meet those opportunities with eager readiness. Building on the foundation of a key Bible passage, Ephesians 5:15-17, Kirk explains how we can "make the most of every opportunity" by stewarding every chance we have to fulfill life's purposes. If you succeed in achieving the priorities addressed in this memorable chapter, you will be successful indeed.

Stewarding Every Relationship. Influence: We all have it, but how do we use it? In human relationships, influence must be stewarded consciously and carefully, and the bedrock of that stewardship is integrity. It was true when your mother first said it to you, and it's true today: *Honesty is the best policy.* Mom wasn't quoting a Bible verse, but she was stating a biblical truth that we are wise to remember in every relationship. As believers it is crucial that we live out integrity in all that we say and do. In the 360° stewardship of life, this demands the character of true convictions and the discipline of genuine communication.

Stewarding Every Concern. Life bombards us with concerns of all shapes, sizes and intensities. How can we handle those concerns? Best of all, through prayer. Chapter Four—*Praying With Purpose*—is a brilliant examination of the Disciple's Prayer and the Lord's Prayer (it's not the one you think). Don't miss the insights of this important section.

Stewarding Every Ability. You may sometimes wonder why, but God has put you in charge of stewarding yourself, of managing your life. He wants to be honored in what you do and how you do it; but He leaves the decisions to you. I was personally challenged by this chapter, especially in what Kirk has written about the call of Moses. It made me realize in a fresh new way how God gives to each of us an extraordinary privilege to steward a sacred trust. And, as the Lord asked Moses, He asks each of us, "What is that in your hand?"

Stewarding Every Asset. I imagine that the majority of Christians instantly think of money when they hear the word "stewardship." There seems to be no getting around that perception. However, the fact is, we *shouldn't* try to get around that perception. Stewardship *does* involve our management of money and our generosity with it. Jesus taught parables on this subject and the apostles wrote lengthy passages about it in the New Testament epistles. All of our monetary and material resources are to be dedicated to the Lord and managed for His glory. It is a practical challenge with a spiritual purpose, and it must be handled strategically. I appreciate the way Chapter 6 gives guidance in taking an inventory of our resources (both tangible and intangible) and following a spiritual investment strategy as we steward every asset.

Stewarding Every Commitment. Commitment is the determination to keep running even when you're tempted in a moment of weakness or exhaustion to drift off to the side of the track and let other runners pass by. Commitment is also devotion to what matters, a spiritual fidelity that constantly reminds you of promises to keep and purposes to fulfill. But the inner fire of commitment must be tended, or it can go out. It takes diligent stewardship—stoking the fire and providing the right fuel—to keep commitment burning bright. I assure you, Chapter 7 will compel you to make—and to keep—some important commitments. You'll be inspired to help readily, to give generously, to witness boldly, and to love unconditionally.

Legendary football coach Vince Lombardi understood that winning is the result of a process that begins at the most basic level. Holding up the familiar pigskin, he started each year's spring training with the words, "Men, this is a football." His purpose was to move from the simple to the complex, concentrating on the essential components that lead to success. That is precisely what this insightful book does in guiding us toward a fuller understanding of biblical stewardship. It covers the basics and then builds on that sure foundation. What we gain in the process is a better grasp of *360° Stewardship*. And, ultimately, what we experience is *360° Success*.

I believe that you will be blessed and benefited by this book in an unmistakable way. May God give you a heart to receive this important message.

John C. Maxwell
Atlanta, Georgia

◢ ◢ ◢ ◢

Dr. John C. Maxwell is an internationally-renowned speaker and author of numerous *New York Times* bestsellers. He is the Founder of INJOY Stewardship Services [ISS], a consulting firm that has provided strategic assistance to thousands of churches, helping them raise more than four billion dollars for ministry projects. He is also the Founder & Chairman of EQUIP, a non-profit ministry that is developing over 1.8 million Christian leaders in 110 nations.

INTRODUCTION

~ ~ ~

My friend and mentor John C. Maxwell, author of *The 360°
Leader* and many other bestsellers, has been such an inspiration
to me. It was my great honor to serve with him for 11 eventful
years as we partnered in ministry projects with thousands of
churches across North America. Over the past decade (when
John was in his 50s) I often heard him say that he "wanted to
make a difference with people who wanted to make a difference doing something that makes a difference at a time that
makes a difference." John recently turned 60 and upon reaching that milestone he told me that he had slightly modified that
statement. "Now," he said, "I want to make a difference with *leaders* who want to make a difference doing something that makes
a difference at a time that makes a difference." He explained to
me that the greater impact would be made in influencing leaders who would then influence countless others. As I listened to
him I realized that John was expressing a key principle of stewardship: *Multiplication is better than addition.* By influencing leaders who influence others, John is able to exponentially multiply
the impact of his life.

John's book, *The 360° Leader*, inspired me to begin thinking
about how the 360-degree concept relates to stewardship.

When I hear or read the term *360°* it prompts a number of mental images—a sentry looking in all directions as he stands guard...an airport beacon casting its light in a constant circular pattern...a mother caring for several young children simultaneously. The 360° concept implies all sides, all segments, the circumference, the entirety. 360° stewardship is, therefore, the oversight of every dimension of life. It is all-encompassing.

To be a 360° steward you must wisely, faithfully manage the trust you have been given. That "trust" for which you are responsible is the sum total of all that you are and all that you have. It is a sacred trust because God Himself gave it to you, and His intention is that you steward it in a way that pleases Him and yields the greatest return. He wants you to not merely add, but to multiply.

The 360° stewardship of life demands diligence, focus and determination. It is constant, and you can't put it on "pause." It is a challenge, a struggle, a daily pursuit. As the Apostle Paul wrote to his spiritual son, Timothy: "But you, man of God, flee from all this, and pursue righteousness, godliness, faith, love, endurance and gentleness. Fight the good fight of the faith. Take hold of the eternal life to which you were called when you made your good confession in the presence of many witnesses. In the sight of God, who gives life to everything, and of Christ Jesus, who while testifying before Pontius Pilate made the good confession, I charge you to keep this command without spot or blame until the appearing of our Lord Jesus Christ."[1]

My hope and prayer is that in reading this book you will think deeply on what it means to "pursue righteousness" as a follower of Christ. That is the heart of *360° Stewardship*, and I am blessed to see it personified every day in the lives of extraordinary people with whom I serve at Samaritan's Purse. Ed Morrow is a perfect example. Ed is the director of World Medical Mission, a vital ministry of Samaritan's Purse. Prior to taking his U.S.-based position, Ed worked on the field for 27 years as a missionary in Africa. During one term of service in the Congo, Ed was an official at a missions hospital where a young mother died after giving birth to a boy. Tragically, the newborn was already motherless; and due to troubled family circumstances, he was put up for adoption. Ed and his wife, Hilde, adopted that baby boy and named him "Zawadi"—Swahili for "a gift". Although they already had two biological children, little Zawadi was welcomed into the Morrow home without reservations.

Today, Zawadi Morrow is 20 years old. An accomplished student, he is about to graduate from Appalachian State University. Zawadi is also a gifted musician who has performed both as a pianist and violinist with recognized orchestras and ensembles. He leads a Bible study group on his campus and another at his church. Zawadi recently drove me to the airport and told me his remarkable story. I asked what his greatest challenge in life has been and he answered, "My generation lives a convenient Christianity. My greatest challenge is surrendering to Christ daily, not letting the things of the world creep in and steal my passion for the Lord. I want to live a consecrated life in front of my peers." As this impressive young man pulled to the curbside and dropped me off, I thought about the 360° stewardship of Ed and Hilde as they loved and raised this "gift" from God. What a legacy!

When Solomon was given the opportunity to ask the Lord for anything he desired, he asked for wisdom. Only with wisdom could he practice 360° stewardship, and because Solomon's desire was pure the Lord blessed him richly. "So God said to him, 'Since you have asked for this and not for long life or wealth for yourself, nor have asked for the death of your enemies but for discernment in administering justice, I will do what you have asked. I will give you a wise and discerning heart, so that there will never have been anyone like you, nor will there ever be."[2] Because he asked for the right thing with the right heart, Solomon became both the wisest and the richest man in all of human history.

What do you ask for of this life? What is the desire that drives you, the passion that motivates you to get up and face every day? As I consider these questions, I think of my children. I am so proud of them, so thrilled about their devotion to Christ and their hearts full of hope in Him. Our oldest child and only daughter, Ashley, was recently married to Julio, and they have already begun an international ministry together. While I was officiating the wedding ceremony I said, "Julio, I have loved Ashley since the day she was born. As a father I have cared for her with a sense of responsibility and a spirit of sacrifice. Will you love her as her mother and I have, will you honor her, sacrifice for her, provide for her, protect her, be with her in good times and bad, in sickness and in health, and will you keep yourself pure for her as long as you live?" I will never forget the sight of Julio's tear-streaked face as he looked into my eyes and replied, "I will...with all my heart."

Our second-born, Clinton, is such a fine young man, and he has already proven himself to be a strong and principled leader. Clint serves as a youth pastor in one of America's largest and most innovative ministries, Northpoint Church in Atlanta. He and his wife, Angela, have been partners in ministry since before they were married; and (best of all) they've blessed us with our first grandchild! Denise and I are grateful for that, but most of all we thank God that Clint and Angela are above everything else dedicated to serving Jesus Christ, stewarding their gifts for His purpose. They have a deep, abiding faith, and I believe that with God's enablement they are going far!

Matthew is the youngest of our children, now in his mid-20s and about to begin his third year of service with Samaritan's Purse (SP) in Sudan—one of the world's most dangerous and difficult places. As I write these words, I have just returned from visiting with Matt and seeing his work firsthand. I had been on a three-week trip to Africa where I met with scores of SP team members in Kenya, Uganda and Sudan. What a privilege to spend time with such amazing people, and what a joy to be able to spend a few of those days with Matt in the place where he is making such an impact. Matt and his teams are responsible for the Church Reconstruction Project (CRP) in Southern Sudan. These remarkable men are rebuilding churches destroyed by the Muslim-dominated Government of Sudan forces over the past decade. Matt and his fellow CRP leaders and team members will soon have rebuilt 80 churches and constructed a large Pastor's Training School in middle Sudan. I was so proud of what Matt has accomplished and I found it very difficult to leave him. As our small plane rumbled down the dirt strip and soared into the sky I looked out the window and saw Matt standing there, waving his hat and saying good-bye. The emotion in my heart flowed from my eyes. Each brief opportunity I have to see him I want the time to be purposeful and the words to count. Matt's life has reminded me how important it is to not waste a single day, and to always choose eternal things over earthly things.

Paul wrote in the concluding verses of 1 Timothy, "Command those who are rich in this present world not to be arrogant nor to put their hope in wealth, which is so uncertain, but to put their hope in God, who richly provides us with everything for our enjoyment. Command them to do good, to be rich in good deeds, and to be generous and willing to share. In this way they will lay up treasure for themselves as a firm foundation for the coming age, so that they may take hold of the life that is truly life."[3] Those words say so much about *360° Stew-*

ardship because in the final analysis it's about all that we do to "take hold of the life that is truly life." I encourage you to read these chapters with an open heart, an open mind and a willingness to steward everything you have and everything you are for the sake of Jesus Christ and His kingdom.

Yours for the Gospel,

Kirk Nowery

Psalm 126:5-6

CHAPTER
ONE
~ ~ ~

CARPE DIEM
Stewarding Every Day

Parkinson's.

A mere mention of the name brings images to the mind:

The still youthful face of Michael J. Fox, now twitching oddly in uncontrollable spasms.

The once potent hands of Muhammad Ali, now trembling and weak with the slightest effort.

For most people, these are the most prominent faces of Parkinson's, a disease that ravages the body with slow and unrelenting cruelty. But when I think of Parkinson's, I see another face: the gently smiling countenance of my own mother. I think back over the 31 years that she endured the endless torture of this sickness as it robbed her strength and stamina bit-by-bit, day-by-day until all the reserves were gone. A few years ago we laid Mom to rest near the small town in South Carolina where she entered this world over 75 years ago. She had a full life; and even though her final three decades were punctuated with pain, she never complained. Each day to her was a gift, a treasure from God to be admired, appreciated and used to please Him. As I contemplate what it means to steward every day, I think first of

Mom because it was at her knee that I learned to value and use each day wisely.

God's Timely Invention

Philosophers over the ages have pondered the subject of time, ever striving to grasp its meaning. Many of them, of course, failed to recognize the most basic fact about time—that it was an invention of God. When He made this physical world, God created the sun and moon to distinguish day and night and, as Genesis explains, to "serve as signs to mark seasons and days and years."[1] Time is a relative marker for our lives but it has no constraints upon God because He is infinitely above it and beyond it. We need time markers, but God does not. In the eloquent prayer of Moses, the great prophet said, "For a thousand years in your sight are like a day that has just gone by, or like a watch in the night."[2]

The eminent theologian Francis Schaeffer often used the following diagram to illustrate as simply as possible the relevance of time to God.

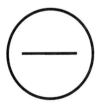

The circle represents God in His eternal oneness. The line, suspended as it is within the circle, represents time. As sovereign over all, God's perspective on time is not limited in any way.

He can view time at any moment of any era. As finite beings, we presently live within time; but He does not, and God is therefore not bound by the seasons and days and years of our earthly existence.

The "Eternal Now" of God

C. S. Lewis, one of the greatest Christian thinkers of the past century, offered this perspective on God's relationship to time: "To Him all the physical events and all the human acts are present in an eternal Now. The liberation of finite wills and the creation of the whole material history of the universe (related to the acts of those wills in all the necessary complexity) is to Him a single operation. In this sense God did not create the universe long ago but creates it at this minute—at every minute."[3]

> *"Humans live in time and therefore attend chiefly to two things: to Eternity itself and to the Present. For the Present is the point at which time touches Eternity"*
>
> —C. S. Lewis

I will be very frank with you and admit that the writings of C. S. Lewis often make my brain ache! The depth of his ideas causes me to think long and hard, and I frequently will read one of his sentences or paragraphs several times. But I find that it's worth the effort because God gave him a remarkable understanding of biblical truths. In his famous book, *The Screwtape Letters*, in addressing this same subject, Lewis wrote, "Humans live in time and therefore attend chiefly to two things: to Eternity itself and to the Present. For the Present is the point at which time touches Eternity."[4]

Rightly Numbering Our Days

We who are believers in Jesus Christ have received through Him the free gift of eternal life. Because we have eternal life, we do not see this life as the sum of our existence. From God's Word we take assurance in the fact that "our citizenship is in heaven"[5] and that life there is our ultimate destination. However, while we're here on earth, living in the dimension of time and space, it is imperative that we make the most of our days as each moment of our Present touches Eternity. The words of the ancient psalm are as relevant to us today as they were thousands of years ago: "Lord...Teach us to number our days aright, that we may gain a heart of wisdom."[6]

To rightly number our days is to allot our time wisely, to live in a way that pleases God and accomplishes His purposes. But what does it mean, and how do we do it? Where do we look for a pattern to follow? The solution is not to buy a new Daytimer® or Franklin-Covey Planner® (though that may be a good idea). No, the first thing to do is to look to Jesus, to examine His life and determine how He spent His time. Obviously, this means we must look to the Scriptures, searching the pages of God's Word for timeless principles of time management.

Doing the Work of the Father

Have you ever examined how Jesus spent His days? Have you analyzed His attitudes towards time? It is clear from the Gospels that in the stewardship of His days Jesus was never worried or hurried. There was never a sense of panic, never a moment of remorse for time lost. He was in all instances and in all circumstances doing the work of the Father, yet never displayed the classic symptoms of a workaholic, so driven by purpose and absorbed by productivity that He forgot about people. In the years of His earthly ministry, Jesus spent time praying, teaching, helping, healing and interacting continually with men and women from all strata of society. But before that public ministry began, Jesus spent 30 years as a carpenter in the obscure village of Nazareth. We really have no idea how He spent his days there; but the implication of Scripture is that He was simply working like anyone else, His identity as Messiah virtually unknown. So, was He wasting time during those silent years? Of course not! In the cosmic calendar known only to God, those 30 years of quiet preparation enabled the three years of intensive, unprecedented service that we read about in the four Gospels.

Jesus...was never so driven by purpose and absorbed by productivity that He forgot about people.

Jesus never became fixated on activity at the expense of the right attitude. In fact, His activity was always governed by His attitude. In writing to the Philippians, the apostle Paul expressed the essence of Jesus in this way:

> "Your attitude should be the same as that of Christ Jesus: Who, being in very nature God, did not consider equality with God something to be grasped, but made himself nothing, taking the very nature of a servant, being made in human likeness. And being found in

> appearance as a man, he humbled himself and
> became obedient to death—even death on a
> cross! Therefore God exalted him to the
> highest place and gave him the name that is
> above every name, that at the name of Jesus
> every knee should bow, in heaven and on
> earth and under the earth, and every tongue
> confess that Jesus Christ is Lord, to the glory
> of God the Father."[7]

Paul says that the attitude of Jesus should be our attitude as well. But how in the world is that possible? Fortunately, the answer is spelled out clearly in the verses immediately following Paul's lofty description of Christ's attitude. And each point he makes is an essential element of the 360° stewardship of every day. Paul gives three specific and easy-to-remember instructions on this subject. Let's take a thorough look at each one...

> "Continue to work out your salvation with
> fear and trembling, for it is God who works in
> you to will and to act according to his good
> purpose."[8]

Work Out Your Salvation. First, to allay any misunderstandings, this statement does not mean to work *for* your salvation. It is not implying in any way that we can save ourselves. The idea that salvation can be earned is a tempting notion, something that appeals to the human ego. We've all met people who say, "I never accept anything I haven't earned." But this is totally untrue, of course. Every one of us has been accepting unearned, undeserved blessings and benefits since the day we were born.

The verb that is translated "work out" in our English Bible is from a Greek term that means, "to work to full completion." It's the word we would use to communicate "working a field" or "working a math problem." But the true key to understanding this passage is the phrase which says, "For it is God who works in you." When you receive Christ, God begins to work in you. His working *in* you then enables you to work *for* Him. It is vital to understand that we're in this together, that we have a viable connection to Christ. That relationship is underscored by one biblical metaphor after another: we are clay, we are branches, we are vessels, we are ambassadors, we are soldiers, we are watchmen, we are servants. Notice that every one of these implies responsibility — a responsibility to yield fully to Christ and to live in absolute obedience to Him.

> *When you receive Christ, God begins to work in you. His working* in *you then enables you to work for* Him.

"Do everything without complaining or arguing, so that you may become blameless and pure, children of God without fault in a crooked and depraved generation, in which you shine like stars in the universe."[9]

Shine Out Your Testimony. If you ever have any doubt as to whether we live in a crooked and depraved generation, just a few minutes browsing through the headlines on CNN or Fox News will remove any uncertainties. And if you turn on the television to MTV you will be even more convinced. The values of this world have been twisted and distorted by the effects of sin, but the Christian measures life by the straight line of God's unfailing Word. Being "without fault" doesn't mean we are perfect but that we belong to Someone who is. And in this world, darkened as it is by impurities of all kinds, we are able to shine as bright lights. We are to be witnesses in this world, communicators who shine out a testimony of God's grace and hope.

> "...as you hold out the word of life—in order that I may boast on the day of Christ that I did not run or labor for nothing."[10]

Hold Out the Word of Life. God has spoken. He has given His Word. And His Word is of such power that it can create something out of nothing and give life to that which is dead. It is this transformational truth that we hold out to a completely secularized society that is estranged from God and ignorant of His principles. Only a Christian who is anchored in the Word can stand against the tide and hold out the Word of Life in a world like ours. But determination by itself is not enough; we must also have the energizing power of God's Spirit working in us. Jesus told His disciples, "As the Father has sent me, so send I you."[11] And so we go, in His name and with His authority.

Only a Christian who is anchored in the Word can stand against the tide and hold out the Word of Life in a world like ours.

Key Elements in Stewarding Every Day

Working out your salvation, shining out your testimony and holding out the Word of Life are three key elements in stewarding every day. They are foundational to the wise, purposeful management of our earthly life. Traditional approaches to time management deal with segmentation, prioritization, implementation and the like; but the bigger question when it comes to time management is not the degree of practical efficiency but the measure of spiritual effectiveness. If we are to be truly wise stewards we have to ask: What is really going to matter at the end of our earthly days? When we stand before God to answer for our lives, what will be of greatest value?

Our highest priority is to be just like our Lord, giving ourselves wholeheartedly in service. None of us knows what tomorrow will bring, so there is no room for bold predictions. As James warned: "Now listen, you who say, 'Today or tomorrow we will go to this or that city, spend a year there, carry on business and make money.' Why, you do not even know what will happen tomorrow."[12] And then James says something even more sobering: "What is your life? You are a mist that appears for a little while and then vanishes. Instead, you ought to say, 'If it is the Lord's will, we will do this or that.' As it is, you boast and brag. All such boasting is evil. Anyone, then, who knows the good he ought to do and doesn't do it, sins."[13] While preaching on this passage of Scripture, Dr. Martin Luther King Jr. once said, "We must use our time creatively, forever realizing that the time is always right to do right."

The Measure of a Life

The measure of a life, from God's perspective, is not determined by its length but by its depth. In the final judgment (and there will be a final judgment), what will matter most is the depth of our devotion to God—how we stewarded our days in faithful service to Him, for Him and in His name. The actual number of our years is irrelevant, a mere speck in the ocean of eternity. Whether we live to age 33 or to 103, our life span is, as James said, "a mist that appears for a little while and then vanishes." This doesn't mean that we cease to exist, but that our existence moves into an entirely new realm, a heavenly realm. But before we reach that point, before the moment comes for us to literally be with the Lord, we must live this life to the full. We must "redeem the time"—wisely investing the hours of each day.

Depth of devotion does not imply some kind of somber, monastic lifestyle. Devotion can be expressed at every level and in every activity of life.

Depth of devotion does not imply some kind of somber, monastic lifestyle. Devotion can be expressed at every level and in every activity of life. As Paul reminded the Corinthians, "Whether you eat or drink or whatever you do, do it all for the glory of God."[14] It is spiritually liberating and empowering to realize that everything—even the most mundane tasks—can be dedicated to God. Our hearts can be set on Him while our hands are set on the work we must do. In the Lord's eyes, there is no difference in value between the work of a surgeon and the work of a servant. It all comes down to a matter of motive: are we serving Him or serving ourselves? Are we seeking His glory or our gratification? The dichotomy between secular and sacred is a man-made division. To God, everything in our lives is sacred—sacred in the sense that it can be and must be devoted to Him.

The Source of Satisfaction

The 360° stewardship of time is a practical challenge, something that demands constant decisions about what to do. This is why we make lists and keep day-planners, and this can be a good thing so long as one does not become a prisoner of the planner. The best advice I can offer on the subject of time management is to choose a strategy, test it in the context of your own roles and responsibilities, and as long as it works, stay with it. If it doesn't work, repeat the process until you find the system that adapts to you (rather than one to which you have to conform). I have used all kinds of methods over the years, but I've learned that no matter what system I'm using I have to remind myself every day that I'm "spending" time: it is a commodity to be spent, just like money, and it must be valued as such. However, I must also remember the bottom-line truth: "This is the day that the Lord has made, I will rejoice and be glad in it."[15] The source of true happiness and satisfaction is not found in a program but in a Person, and it comes to the steward who lives to do the Master's will.

There is a compelling story in the Gospel of Luke about an event that occurred when Jesus was teaching in one of the synagogues.[16] His attention was drawn to a woman who was bent over and unable to stand straight. The Bible says that she "had been crippled by a spirit for eighteen years." Jesus called her forward and said to her, "Woman, you are set free from your infirmity."[17] Then He put His hands on her and she immediately straightened up and began to praise God. Seeing this happen, the ruler of the synagogue became indignant because Jesus had healed someone on the Sabbath day. He said to the people who were present: "There are six days for work. So come and be healed on those days, not on the Sabbath."[18] He was clueless about the absurdity of his words until Jesus responded: "You hypocrites! Doesn't each of you on the Sabbath untie his ox or donkey from the stall and lead it out to give it water? Then should not this woman, a daughter of Abraham, whom Satan has kept bound for eighteen long years, be set free on the Sabbath day from what bound her?"[19] And the story concludes: "When he had said this, all of his opponents were humiliated, but the people were delighted with all the wonderful things he was doing."[20]

Jesus' bold and compassionate act challenged their understanding of God's priorities.

The so-called religious leaders were concerned about compliance with a system—a system that had elevated the importance of a particular day to a level far beyond what God ever intended. In their minds, they were exercising the correct stewardship of their days; however, in their system certain days had become more important than people, and adherence to the rules took precedence over profound human needs. Jesus' bold and compassionate act challenged their understanding of God's priorities. Jesus was telling them that if we truly love God we will truly love people, and we will do whatever it takes to steward our moments and days in a way that communicates that love. If we keep this in mind, and if we keep our eyes on Him, we can steward every day in a manner that is truly purposeful.

CHAPTER
TWO

~ ~ ~

RAPID RESPONSE
Stewarding Every Opportunity

I hate to miss an opportunity, and that day I missed a big one.

My lifelong friend, David Janney, called me and said, "Kirk, I want you go somewhere with me today."

"Where do you want to go?" I replied with a sense of hesitation, since I never know what he has up his sleeve.

"Germany," he said. And he stated it with the ease that one might have in saying, "I'm going to the mall."

"Germany!" I said. "Why in the world do you want me to go to Germany with you? And why do we have to do it today?"

"We have to go today," he answered, "because they're tearing down the Berlin Wall, and we have to see it. This is a once-in-a-lifetime opportunity, Kirk. There's only one Berlin Wall, and once it's down, it's down."

I instantly knew that he was right, but I came up with so many excuses—meetings I had to attend, church services I had to plan, counseling sessions I had to conduct—and although I could have delegated, rescheduled or changed everything that was pending, I chose the path most traveled and I turned down the opportunity.

"Man, that would be a phenomenal thing to see," I told him, "but I just can't get away right now."

He tried a bit harder to convince me, but I still said 'No'— and I have regretted that decision for more than a decade and a half. Whenever I see images of those thousands of people in a frenzy of freedom, bashing away at that despised wall with sledgehammers and picks and whatever else they could get their hands on, I wish that I had been there. I wish that I could have seen it firsthand. But I missed an opportunity because I chose to do the expected rather than the extraordinary.

I missed an opportunity because I chose to do the expected rather than the extraordinary.

The Expected vs. The Extraordinary

Three years later, my friend David called and once again said, "Kirk, I want you to go somewhere with me." And before he was able to tell me where we were going, I said, "When are we leaving?" I wasn't about to miss another chance to experience something of lasting significance. He was startled by the quickness of my reply, but he recovered quickly and said, "It's a good thing you're so determined to go because where we're going is so unstable right now that we can't even get confirmed visas to enter the country. This is going to be an adventure." His cautions did not deter me. I was certain about this decision.

Our destination was Albania, a relatively small nation in

southeastern Europe, bordered by Greece, Yugoslavia and Macedonia. Since 1944, Albania had been under communist rule, the staunchest member of the Soviet bloc. For more than 40 years, Enver Hoxha ruled Albania with a ruthless disregard for human life. An avowed Stalinist, Hoxha confiscated farmland and commercial enterprises and established a totalitarian state. Untold thousands of people were killed for opposing his government, and thousands more were sent to internment camps and prisons. In 1967, Hoxha proclaimed Albania the world's first completely atheist nation. Following his death in the late 1980s, Albania was in complete disarray, a pathetic example of the folly of communism. A short time later, the USSR began to disintegrate and Christian missionaries began to enter the newly-freed eastern European nations. But Albania had become so isolated that no one knew what was happening there. We were about to find out.

Walking into Albania's capital city, Tirana, was like stepping back in time. It looked like the faded image from a World War II history book. Nearly all the vehicles were from the 1940s and the city was drab and lifeless. I noticed that countless windows were covered with cloth, paper, cardboard—anything that would keep out the cold. Just before his death, the madman Hoxha had ordered the army to break all the windows and destroy caches of food. The people looked shell-shocked, and they were clearly malnourished.

After getting a room at Tirana's only hotel, we began to explore the city. Along the way, we met a young lady who spoke English and she agreed to serve as our interpreter. Everywhere we went there was a buzz of conversation. The word was out that some Americans had come to town. Albanian military officers stopped us repeatedly and "fined" us for one infraction or another. We had pockets full of coins, so we would pay the equivalent of 10 or 15 cents and then be waved on. Every one of those young soldiers we met had an emptiness in his eyes. We left the center of town and began to wander down a side street. The scene that confronted us is one I will never forget.

A large number of people were crowded around some kind of compound. The stone wall surrounding the property could not be climbed over because jagged pieces of glass had been cemented into the top of the wall—a Third World version of barbed wire. But disregarding the danger, people were handing children over that wall! We made our way through the crowd and reached the front gate of the compound. Seeing that we were foreigners, the military police opened the gate and let us in. Once inside those forbidding walls we looked around us and saw a sea of children. We realized: *This is why God sent us here. This is an opportunity from Him.*

We were ushered to the main building where nurses greeted us with tears streaming down their faces. They spoke to us excitedly and urgently in their own language. Following a small group of nurses, we were shown one dimly-lit room after another, and in each one we saw children from wall to wall. Hundreds of precious children stared up at us, their dark eyes seeming to plead with us for attention. The nurses were crying and talking very rapidly, and our interpreter was doing her best to translate as quickly as possible. "We need help...please help us...we have been waiting for you to come...thank God you are here...." We kept moving through the building, confronted everywhere with the sight of children. On the fourth floor, at the top of the stairs, lying on mats strewn across the floor were scores of babies, each wrapped papoose-style in rough burlap fabric. It was difficult to keep our composure.

What in the world could we do here? We were just two guys from South Florida, best friends since childhood, both of us now pastoring churches. How could we respond to something so overwhelming?

The nurses took us to the basement, a damp, cave-like room that was nearly empty. The wood supply for the furnace was just about gone. The medicine cabinet was bare. The large refrigerator contained a block of cheese, some hard bread and one container of rancid milk. It was all they had left.

We looked around us and saw a sea of children... We realized: This is why God sent us here. This is an opportunity from Him.

How could we make a difference? As teenagers we had once worked as volunteers in an orphanage; but this was almost too much to take in. We returned to our hotel to get our bearings, but soon the ring of an ancient phone sounded through the lobby. A few seconds later, David was asked to speak to someone on the phone. He stepped over to the desk to take the call, and after a very brief conversation returned to where I was standing. "Well," he said, "they're coming to pick us up. We're going to meet the new President of Albania."

Responding Rapidly...with Help and Hope

Within minutes we were picked up and taken with a full police escort to the presidential palace. Once inside we were greeted by President Sali Berisha and an entire entourage of officials. The president was curious as to why we had come and what we were doing in his country. While I was still mentally processing the question, David answered, "We represent World Hope, and we're here to help the children." I looked at him and thought, *World Hope? What is World Hope?* We're just two guys backed up by two churches and a few friends!

The President was thrilled that Americans had finally come to his country, and he was appreciative that we wanted to help the suffering children. Within a couple of days he had given us the responsibility for the orphanage in Tirana and orphanages in four other cities. In our hotel lobby we put up a sign that read:

WORLD HOPE
Room #112
Changing the World
One Child at a Time

Over the next two weeks we met with a constant stream of government officials and orphanage personnel. We were even successful in coordinating the emergency delivery of an entire planeload of food, medicine and relief supplies (paid for by U.S. Foreign Aid). There was, without exaggeration, one miracle after another as God made provision for an extraordinary situation. And there we were, just being His ambassadors in a place so desperately in need of His life-giving power. In the process,

God gave birth to a ministry that is now touching lives on every continent. Its name, World Hope, was coined on the spur of the moment—but its impact has been long-lasting. A golden opportunity was stewarded, and since then God has given many, many more.

I'm grateful for the ways in which David Janney has lived out the truths of 360° stewardship. Because of his shining example, I have gained a world of understanding about what it means to give hope to people in desperate need. When David and I were both serving as pastors of large churches—he in Orlando and I in Miami—he would urge me to go with him to the "remotest parts of the earth"—not because he was into taking trips but because he was into meeting challenges. Looking back, I can't believe I turned down the invitations, each time convincing myself that it was better to not get involved. I realize now that I didn't grasp my role and my church's part in fulfilling the Great Commission of Jesus Christ. David's persistence finally broke through my stubbornness and brought me to a whole new level of spiritual awareness. He has gone on to build World Hope into a significant organization, and his plan to establish "Hope Centers" in strategic places of need is making a difference in thousands of lives. I have just returned from a visit to the Hope Center in Nairobi, Kenya—a place where Christ-centered education, leadership development, medical care,

I realize now that I didn't grasp my role and my church's part in fulfilling the Great Commission of Jesus Christ. David's persistence finally broke through my stubbornness.

water purification and the feeding of hungry children happens every day. In that remarkable place, as in all the other Hope Centers, David and his team are "making the most of every opportunity."

I have the remarkable privilege of serving today as Chief Operating Officer of Samaritan's Purse, one of the world's most extensive relief and development ministries. Samaritan's Purse (SP) has thousands of dedicated team members serving in over 100 nations around the globe. When a disaster strikes, or when a crisis erupts—at home or abroad—SP is ready to respond. Our president, Franklin Graham, often says, "When there is a desperate situation, the first hand to reach out to people in need should be the hand of Jesus—and we are that hand." One example of SP's commitment to this priority is the Billy Graham Rapid Response ministry, a multi-discipline team that intercedes in times of urgent need. As I write these words, tragedy has paralyzed the campus of Virginia Tech University, where a madman brutally murdered over 30 students and faculty. Within the first hour after the news broke, the Billy Graham Rapid Response team was mobilized with over 25 crisis counselors who are converging to provide spiritual guidance on the Virginia Tech campus.

> *"When there is a desperate situation, the first hand to reach out to people in need should be the hand of Jesus—and we are that hand."*
>
> *—Franklin Graham*

The concept of "rapid response" resonates with me as I reflect on what it means to steward every opportunity. As I look back to that amazing time in Albania and as I think of the far-reaching work of Samaritan's Purse, my heart is drawn to Ephesians 5:15-17. In the entire Bible, those verses for me are the most relevant on this subject. Take a moment and meditate on this admonition from the apostle Paul:

> "Be very careful, then, how you live—not as unwise but as wise, making the most of every opportunity, because the days are evil. Therefore do not be foolish, but understand what the Lord's will is."[1]

Let's explore the meaning of one phrase in particular: *"making the most of every opportunity, because the days are evil."* As we run life's race, we come across one opportunity after another; but we also encounter all sorts of obstacles along the way. The challenge is to gain the greatest value from the opportunities while avoiding or overcoming the obstacles. While he was in Ephesus, Paul sent a letter to the Corinthians describing an opportunity he had been given and the obstacles that came with it. He wrote: "But I will stay on at Ephesus until Pentecost, because a great door for effective work has opened to me, and there are many who oppose me."[2]

Paul was not intimidated by the fact that he had enemies bent on discrediting or even destroying him. He found confidence and great courage in the certainty that God had given him an opportunity for effective ministry, and he was determined to maximize that opportunity. That was the pattern of his entire life from the point of his conversion to the day he died as a martyr for Jesus Christ. Paul practiced the 360° stewardship of opportunities—he seized every chance he was given to declare God's truth, to demonstrate God's character and to encourage God's people. However, as he wrote on several occasions, he was able to make the most of his opportunities not because he was a great saint but because he was a humble servant. He never considered himself as one who had "arrived" at a state of total spiritual maturity. Instead, he kept pressing forward, redeeming the opportunities each step of the way. As he wrote to the Philippians, "I press on to take hold of that for which Christ Jesus took hold of me. Brothers, I do not consider myself yet to have taken hold of it. But one thing I do: Forgetting what is behind and straining toward what is ahead, I press on toward the goal to win the prize for which God has called me heavenward in Christ Jesus."[3]

As I read God's Word, I see other believers who, like Paul, show the importance of wisely stewarding God-given opportunities. I think of Joshua, who had spent 40 years in the wilderness as second-in-command to Moses, finally fulfilling the opportunity to lead the nation of Israel across the Jordan and into the land of promise. I think of Esther, who made the most of her opportunity to influence the king and save her people from certain genocide. I think of Nehemiah, who received news of a crisis, but saw it as an opportunity, and against all odds led the Jewish people of Jerusalem to rise up and rebuild the walls that guarded their city. We could study in depth any of these remarkable individuals, but I direct your attention instead to another person who demonstrated the stewardship of opportunity in a truly memorable way. Her name was Deborah, which means "one who seeks." When we examine her life we see someone who was always seeking God's will and seizing opportunities to bring Him honor.

Opportunity and the Power of Intuition

I have always been intrigued by the expression, "a woman's intuition." It isn't in the Bible, but I'm sure it's real. The evidence is undeniable that God blesses women with an intuitive ability that sometimes borders on the astonishing. A woman's intuition is often superior to a man's cold reasoning (or his pig-headedness, as the case may be). A lady once told me that if Pontius Pilate had taken the advice of his wife he would not have signed the death warrant for Jesus! She had a point, and I couldn't argue against it. I must admit that I have learned a great deal from the intuition of my mother, my wife, my daughter and a number of other significant women. In essence, they have taught me lessons in the 360° stewardship of opportunity, because one of its major components is intuition. You can't seize an opportunity if you don't perceive that one is there.

A lady once told me that if Pontius Pilate had taken the advice of his wife he would not have signed the death warrant for Jesus!

Deborah was blessed with a mighty portion of God-given intuition. She had flawless expertise as a leader, and God chose her to be one of the judges of Israel. She could read situations, read people and recognize opportunities. Judges 4:5 says, "She held court under the Palm of Deborah between Ramah and

Bethel in the hill country of Ephraim, and the Israelites came to her to have their disputes settled." In that era, palm trees were very rare in Palestine, so the tree itself was symbolic of Deborah's uncommon gifts and abilities. She matched intuition with inspiration as she poured out wisdom to everyone who sought her counsel.

Deborah's sphere of influence included everyone from peasants to kings. But with each person she stewarded the opportunity to give valued insight. From the shade of that palm tree, she confidently guided her nation, successfully resolving conflicts and rendering wise judgments. God blessed Deborah with prophetic knowledge of the military strategies Israel was to employ in battling their enemies.

Deborah's sphere of influence included everyone from peasants to kings. But with each person she stewarded the opportunity to give valued insight.

On one occasion she sent for Barak, an Israelite commander from Naphtali. She said to him: "The Lord, the God of Israel, commands you: 'Go, take with you ten thousand men of Naphtali and Zebulun and lead the way to Mount Tabor. I will lure Sisera, the commander of Jabin's army, with his chariots and his troops to the Kishon River and give him into your hands.'"[4]

Barak, although he was a brave man, was not as brave as Deborah. He said to her, "If you go with me I will go; but if you don't go with me, I won't go."[5] Rather than argue with him or try to convince him to change his mind, Deborah accepted Barak's reply and taught him an unforgettable lesson in the 360° stewardship of opportunities. He would soon learn that an opportunity to exercise great power (such as he was given) is first an opportunity to exercise great faith. He should have known to take Deborah at her word and to seize the golden moment that he had been given. After all, she was speaking not her own word, but God's. Barak would still have a measure of success, but he would not experience the total success that would have been his through wholehearted faith.

"'Very well,' Deborah said, 'I will go with you. But because of the way you are going about this, the honor will not be yours, for the Lord will hand Sisera over to a woman.' So Deborah went with Barak to Kedesh, where he summoned Zebulun and Naphtali. Ten thousand men followed him, and Deborah also went with him."[6]

Opportunity and the Value of Inspiration

For all we know, Barak may have thought that Deborah was going to be the woman who would get the credit for total victory. But God had something else in mind. After the enemy forces had assembled in a massive front along the Kishon River, Deborah said to Barak, "Go! This is the day the Lord has given Sisera into your hands. Has not the Lord gone ahead of you?"[7] Like a fearless general, she shouted the command for engagement and the battle ensued. Inspired by Deborah's stirring words, Barak led the charge. "So Barak went down Mount Tabor, followed by ten thousand men."[8] Imagine what this must have looked like to the enemy. The passage goes on, "At Barak's advance, the Lord routed Sisera and all his chariots and army by the sword, and Sisera abandoned his chariot and fled on foot. But Barak pursued the chariots and army as far as Harosheth Haggoyim." And then the clincher: "All the troops of Sisera fell by the sword; not a man was left."[9]

Yes, it was a total rout; but it was not yet a total victory because Sisera had gotten away. For Barak, the supreme honor of the victory that day would have been to personally capture and slay Sisera. But it was not to be. "Sisera, however, fled on foot to the tent of Jael, the wife of Heber the Kenite, because there were friendly relations between Jabin king of Hazor and the clan of Heber the Kenite."[10] Sisera, the coward, had found what he thought to be a safe house. "Jael went out to meet Sisera and said to him, 'Come, my lord, come right in. Don't be afraid.' So he entered her tent, and she put a covering over him."[11] What a welcome sight for a soldier on the run: a gracious, hospitable woman willing to take him in! "I'm thirsty, he said, please give me some water." The story continues: "She opened a skin of milk, gave him a drink, and covered him up. 'Stand in the doorway of the tent,' he told her. 'If someone comes by and asks you, 'Is anyone here?' say 'No.'"[12] As Sisera gave these all-important instructions, the satisfying warmth of the milk was already starting to make him feel relaxed. He was already completely worn out, and soon he was fast asleep on the floor of Jael's tent.

Opportunity and the Importance of Initiative

Jael had a 360° understanding of the situation and was inspired by the opportunity that God had brought right into her own tent. She immediately took the initiative. The Bible says that "Jael, Heber's wife, picked up a tent peg and a hammer and went quietly to him while he lay fast asleep, exhausted. She drove the peg through his temple into the ground, and he died."[13] It was a gruesome scene, no doubt. But God had used a cagey woman to execute judgment on an enemy of His chosen people. We can only imagine the wily expression on her face when she broke the news to the Israelites. "Barak came by in pursuit of Sisera, and Jael went out to meet him. 'Come,' she said, 'I will show you the man you're looking for.' So he went in with her, and there lay Sisera with the tent peg through his temple— dead."[14] The passage concludes with these words: "On that day God subdued Jabin, the Canaanite king, before the Israelites. And the hand of the Israelites grew stronger and stronger against Jabin, the Canaanite king, until they destroyed him."[15]

Jael saw the opportunity and did not hesitate; and God used her as a key figure in a great victory. The Song of Deborah celebrates her initiative.

Jael saw the opportunity and did not hesitate; and God used her as a key figure in a great victory. Some would condemn her act as cold-blooded murder, but the Song of Deborah in Judges chapter 5 celebrates her initiative: "Most blessed of women be Jael, the wife of Heber the Kenite, most blessed of tent-dwelling women."[16] Barak, on the other hand, was actually rebuked by the fact that God had used Jael. His conditional obedience to the Lord brought conditional honor from the Lord. But Deborah received the highest blessing from God, because she had stewarded a great opportunity with great wisdom and absolute faith. In the final stanza of her song, Deborah says, "So may all your enemies perish, O Lord! But may they who love you be like the sun when it rises in its strength."[17] Then the chapter concludes with this powerful statement: "Then the land had peace forty years."[18] In a time of great calamity and chaos, peace came to Israel through the leadership of a godly woman who stewarded wisely and made the most of every opportunity.

Now, let's bring this down to where we live. What are the opportunities that we are called upon to steward as believers of the 21st century? As I look back at the opportunities God has already given me (and for which I must one day answer to Him), I see that so many of them fall into three categories: Opportunities to communicate God's message; Opportunities to express God's love; and Opportunities to act in God's power. In each of these categories are priorities that I am convinced apply to every Christian.

Peace came to Israel through the leadership of a godly woman who stewarded wisely and made the most of every opportunity.

Stewarding Opportunities to Communicate God's Message

Think for a moment about the last words Jesus spoke to His disciples before He ascended back to heaven: "But you will receive power when the Holy Spirit comes on you; and you will be my witnesses in Jerusalem, and in all Judea and Samaria, and to the ends of the earth."[19] A few days before He made that dramatic, final statement, Jesus had said to them, "All authority in heaven and on earth has been given to me. Therefore go and make disciples of all nations, baptizing them in the name of Father and of the Son and of the Holy Spirit, and teaching them to obey everything I have commanded you. And surely I will be with you always, to the very end of the age."[20]

The "end of the age" as Jesus calls it is the end of the Church Age, the time from the coming of the Holy Spirit in power to the second coming of Christ in glory. That "age" is now 2,000 years long, and only God knows when it will end; but until it does, those who believe in Him have a crucial mission to fulfill. That mission—which is often called "The Great Commission"—is to evangelize the world and make disciples of Jesus Christ. "Evangel" means "Gospel," and evangelization is the spreading of the Gospel—the Good News of life and salvation through Jesus Christ. It is imperative to communicate this message because unless people put their faith in Christ, they are without hope.

Opportunities to communicate the Gospel ought to be treated as if they were great riches. In fact, they are like great riches to the ones still waiting to hear, still waiting to know that Jesus is the only way, the only truth, the only life. Where and when do these opportunities come to us? They occur on the journey of life...

...in conversation with a friend who is going through a struggle...

...in meeting someone for the first (and perhaps only) time on a plane...

...in discussing eternal life with someone who is soon to reach the end of this earthly life...

...in myriad opportunities that can come as brief snippets of time or in very lengthy and involved relationships.

Sharing the Gospel is an essential part of the Christian life. It is not a matter of personal preference, an "elective" in the school of discipleship. Nor is it a matter of personal performance, as if we by our own efforts lead someone to Christ. The one who actually leads is the Holy Spirit, who draws souls to the Savior. But God has chosen to use us as His messengers in the process. We, the ones who have already found the Bread of Life, must tell everyone else about it. As we live from day to day, God gives us opportunities to sow the seed of His truth. In the questions we answer, in the comments we make, in the opinions we share about a thousand-and-one different things, we can incorporate the truth of the Word and the message of the Gospel. But to seize the opportunities we must be ready. As Peter advised in his first epistle, "Always be prepared to give an answer to everyone who asks you to give the reason for the hope that you have."[21]

Stewarding Opportunities to Express God's Love

To empathize is to put yourself in another person's position—to identify with what they are thinking and feeling. We see this empathy in the beautiful example of the Good Samaritan, who looked upon the wounded man and had compassion on him.[22] The word *compassion* means, literally, "to suffer with another." When we act with true Christian compassion we feel the emotional or spiritual pain of the other person, suffering with them just as Jesus did with all who came to Him for help or healing.

The Samaritan was presented with what we would call a "can't-miss" opportunity to express God's love by rescuing a person in great distress. Two others had the same "can't-miss" opportunity before the Samaritan came along, and yet they missed it completely. Worse yet, they *chose* to miss it, willfully going to the other side of the road to escape the discomfort of getting too close to someone undesirable. They had exactly the same attitude we see today toward the homeless and profoundly poor of our own society. Many of us don't want to see them, much less get close to them and actually do something to lift them up physically, financially or spiritually.

- - -

Two others had the same "can't-miss" opportunity before the Samaritan came along, but they missed it completely. Worse yet, they chose *to miss it.*

- - -

The fact is, people all around us are in need of help and healing, just like the multitudes that Jesus looked upon with such pity that it made Him weep. But we're not just talking about feeling empathy for the down-and-outers; our compassion must extend to every human being with whom we relate, Christians and non-Christians alike. If we're going to be like Jesus, if we're going to practice 360° stewardship and seize the opportunities of life as He did, we must have His attitude—caring for those who are hurting, serving with humility, seeking always to please the Father.

Stewarding Opportunities to Act in God's Power

When we empathize we instinctively feel what another person is feeling. That's what Jesus did constantly as he interacted with people from all walks of life. Of course, He didn't just feel what others were feeling; He profoundly, proactively affected their lives. He felt others' pain and then acted to alleviate that pain. As His followers, we are called to pattern our lives after His example, and the reason we can do this is because we have a resident energy source that He enables us to transmit. As believers, we are indwelled by the Spirit of God: that's where the power comes from. We have a God-given potential to do things that will strengthen those who are weak, not because of our strength but by the energizing power of the Holy Spirit at work in us. We can say the right thing at the right time and give true encouragement, not to manipulate others but to motivate them to trust God.

We have a God-given potential to do things that will strengthen those who are weak, not because of our strength but by the energizing power of the Holy Spirit at work in us.

We also have opportunities to spiritually energize others when we stand for what is right. In an age that is increasingly anti-Christian in its demeanor, we will become more and more conscious of this challenge. But this is nothing new. The verses quoted at the beginning of this chapter bear a second look: "Be very careful, then, how you live—not as unwise but as wise, making the most of every opportunity, because the days are evil."[23] Notice especially the last phrase, "because the days are evil." Can there be any doubt that these are evil days? They are evil because this entire world system, so weighed down with sin and destruction, is against Christ, against the Bible and contrary to all that is good and right. A battle rages, and it will not end until Jesus comes. Until He does, we have opportunities to redeem. As we seize each one, let's remember some of the concluding words of Paul's letter to the Ephesians:

> "Therefore put on the full armor of God, so that when the day of evil comes, you may be able to stand your ground, and after you have done everything, to stand. Stand firm then, with the belt of truth buckled around your waist, with the breastplate of righteousness in place, and with your feet fitted with the readiness that comes from the gospel of peace. In addition to all this, take up the shield of faith, with which you can extinguish all the flaming arrows of the evil one. Take the helmet of salvation and the sword of the Spirit, which is the word of God. And pray in the Spirit on all occasions with all kinds of prayers and requests. With this in mind, be alert and always keep on praying for all the saints."[24]

CHAPTER
THREE
~ ~ ~ ~
# INFLUENCE & IMPACT
Stewarding Every Relationship

Prominently displayed in the Pro Football Hall of Fame in Canton, Ohio, is a life-size bronze bust of Don Shula, legendary head coach of the Baltimore Colts and the Miami Dolphins. Visitors study Shula's rugged features on that sculpture as they read the plaque which recounts his impressive accomplishments. When he concluded his 33rd and final season in 1995, Don Shula was the winningest head coach in NFL history. His teams won the Super Bowl twice; and his 1972 Dolphins achieved the only perfect season ever, finishing with a 17-0 record.

For 11 memorable seasons I had the extraordinary privilege of serving as Chaplain to the Miami Dolphins football team. During those years I had a front-row seat (actually, a sideline bench) that enabled me to see up-close and personal one of the most gifted coaches of our generation—of any generation, in fact. For me, the essence of Don Shula is not captured in a bronze statue or a highlight film, but in the man I observed for those 11 seasons. I count Don Shula as a friend and a gentleman; but I will always think of him foremost as a leader of men.

In conversations with him and in observations of him, I learned so much about how to steward relationships.

Recently I had a conversation with Lyle Blackwood, a star player on the Dolphins team that went to Super Bowl XIX. We were discussing those exciting days and I asked Lyle what stood out most for him when he thought of Shula's leadership. Lyle replied, "The thing that I admired most about Coach Shula was how focused he was when we were in the heat of battle. He was right on the field with us...always using every ounce of influence he had. To be a good coach you have to be like that—to be one with the players and so connected to the game that, even though you are on the sideline, your players are an extension of you and you play through them. I believe that's why Coach didn't mind giving us a piece of his mind on many occasions. He took it personally because he felt like he was in the game with us."

The sphere of influence differs measurably from one person to another, but each of us is influential in very definable ways.

When Lyle shared that, I remembered that Don Shula could be a very difficult man when he was pushing his players to excel. But one phrase in Lyle's comments captures the reason Coach Shula was like that: he was "using every ounce of influence he had" to get the greatest possible result from his teams.

Your Sphere of Influence

When you read or hear the word *influence* perhaps you're prompted to think that it applies to only a select percentage of people; but the fact is that every person exercises influence in personal relationships. The sphere of that influence can differ measurably from one person to another, but each of us is influential in very definable ways. How we use and manage our influence can spell the difference between success and failure—for us and for those whose lives we affect. It is undeniably a 360-degree proposition, and it encompasses all kinds of relationships.

We first learn about influence through a mother's soothing voice and warm embrace. Whatever she says or does affects how we feel and what we think. Through her we experience virtually everything that is foundational to life itself. In her sphere of influence, no one is more important; and we sense it even in our infancy. As one grows older, a mother's influence changes; but it is always there, for good or bad. Some mothers unfortunately cannot bring themselves to adapt wisely to the changes that time and maturity demand. They keep on mothering in a way that fails to properly utilize their influence. Dr. James Dobson tells the story of a friend whose mother had the wisdom to recognize the evolving nature of her influence. After his first hectic week at college, Dobson's friend received a package from home. It was a large, nondescript envelope that contained a strangely shaped object. With great curiosity the young man hurriedly opened the package. Inside was a pair of neatly starched, ironed and folded apron strings. Mom had cut them off and sent them as a symbolic, loving acknowledgement of her son's newfound independence. What a brilliant woman!

In the 360° stewardship of life, relationships are of central importance. You may have an impact in business, art, science, athletics or some field of endeavor; but ultimately and most significantly, your life impacts other lives. You are connected to people, and that connection is of high value. It is what truly matters. As a friend once told me with great intensity, "Kirk, only two things last forever—the Word of God and the souls of human beings." I have never forgotten those words, and I hope I never do. They have challenged me to keep my focus on things eternal—driving me right to the core issue of how I can most effectively steward every relationship.

To fully explore the realm of relationships would require many books, each of them longer and more detailed than this one. And, frankly, others are more qualified than I to write those books. The particular emphasis of this chapter is the uniquely Christian dimension of human relationships. Specifically, I'm going to address three high-priority objectives at stake in the stewardship of relationships. These three priorities have helped me to recognize the importance of...

1. Influencing people to know the One True God.

2. Influencing people to believe and follow Jesus Christ.

3. Influencing people to live a normal Christian life.

The practical outworking of these three purposes is a lifelong challenge, but it is infinitely, immeasurably rewarding.

Influencing People to Know the One True God

It is becoming increasingly unpopular in our secularized culture to suggest that there is one true God. A lot of people get nervous when they hear such a statement because it implies that there are numerous false gods that are being worshiped. And, as is commonly thought, it's just not nice to say bad things about somebody else's god. However, if there is indeed only one true God, and if He has revealed Himself definitively and has confirmed His uniqueness absolutely, we must proclaim it to everyone.

Who is the one true God and what can we say about Him?

He is the God of the Bible. Penned by more than 40 writers on three continents over the span of 1,500 years, the Bible is the Book of Books. By its own testimony, it is the very word of God, an inspired expression of His truth and His character. The Bible does not merely *contain* the words of God, as some contend; it *is* the Word of God; and in its authoritative message God communicates what we need to know *about* Him and how we ought to live *for* Him.

He is Creator and Lord of All. The very first verse of the Bible says, "In the beginning, God created the heavens and the earth."[1] By His command, the universe was spoken into existence. Out of nothing He brought forth everything. This planet and all that it contains was created by Him, and it is all subject to His lordship. "For by him all things were created: things in heaven and on earth, visible and invisible, whether thrones or powers or rulers or authorities; all things were created by him and for him. He is before all things, and in him all things hold together."[2]

He is the Eternal Three-in-One God. In a way that we cannot begin to grasp because it is so far beyond our comprehension, God is three Persons in One. He is God the Father, God the Son and God the Holy Spirit; yet He is One God.

Father...Son...Holy Spirit. When we refer to any or all of these Persons, we are referring to God Himself, not to some concept about Him.

When we refer to any or all of these Persons, we are referring to God Himself, not to some concept about Him. We see His plurality from the very start of the Scriptures when God said, "Let *us* make man in our image...."[3] And we see His three-in-one nature at the baptism of Jesus when the *Father* speaks His approval, the *Son* demonstrates His obedience to the Father, and the *Spirit* comes in confirmation of the divine will.[4]

He is the One and Only Savior of Mankind. The Gospel of John says that the Father so loved sinful mankind that He gave His "only begotten Son" so that we might receive eternal life through Him.[5] That wonderful phrase from the King James version— "only begotten Son"—means that He was the one and only, the unique one who was fully man and yet fully God. He would make salvation possible through His perfect life, sacrificial death and victorious resurrection. God's desire is that we as flawed, sinful human beings, who are incapable of saving ourselves, would put our trust in the person and work of Jesus Christ, the Son of God.

Influencing People to Believe
and Follow Jesus Christ

It's one thing to say that there is one true God. But it's quite another thing to say that there is only one way to know Him. But as Christians, that *is* what we say. Not because we are arrogant or narrow-minded, or because we hold to an antiquated way of thinking. We aren't arrogant, because arrogance is based upon ignorant pride that draws attention to self, as opposed to this belief, which directs attention to God. We aren't narrow-minded, because narrow-mindedness implies a petty and limited range of vision, as opposed to this belief that sees the whole breadth of nature created by one eternal Being. And we don't follow an antiquated way of thinking because that implies that the belief is an obsolete concept, outmoded and discredited as opposed to this belief that is still relevant and even transformational today.

We say as Christians that there is only one way to God because that's what the Bible says: "Salvation is found in no one else, for there is no other name under heaven given to men by which we must be saved."[6] This is a categorical statement that leaves no room whatsoever for flexibility or alternative ideas. If one wants to receive eternal salvation, there is no one else who can give it except Jesus. There is no other name but His name with the authority to give life and give it abundantly. Jesus said to His disciples, "I am the way and the truth and the life. No one comes to the Father except through me."[7]

We are called to communicate to everyone within our sphere of influence that Jesus is the way, the truth and the life. As

His followers, we spread this good news and we witness to the reality of our life in Him. I can tell you without reservation that I have experienced no greater feeling than the joy of leading someone to Christ and seeing that person spiritually transformed. While working on this very chapter, God gave me a marvelous opportunity to share my faith. In a very unusual place, I was able to practice the stewardship of influence as I told someone God's plan of salvation. It happened on a hunting trip near Mt. McKinley, North America's tallest mountain. Mt. McKinley, which soars over 20,000 feet into the Alaskan sky, is called *Denali* by the native tribes. It is a spectacular sight from any perspective, and we had a great view of the mountain from our campsite about 40 miles west of the peak.

Our party was led by two highly experienced hunting guides—great outdoorsmen who are passionate about their work and remarkable in their skill at guiding hunts for mountain sheep, moose and brown bears. I listened with great fascination to their stories of adventure in the wilds of Alaska. When one of them asked me, "Kirk, what do you do for a living?" the whole experience changed instantly for me from hunting expedition to "fishing trip." I say that because when someone asks me what I do, I always take it as an opportunity to be, as Jesus said, a "fisher of men."[8] I told those two burly men how a pastor took the time to come by my house when I was 12 years old to tell me the meaning of John 3:16. I described how he unfolded the truth of that verse which says, "For God so loved the world that he gave his only begotten son, that whosoever believes in him shall not perish but have everlasting life." I recounted how he told me that the word "whosoever" included me. As I went on with my story it was clear that the message was connecting with one of those two men. It was exactly what he had been waiting all his life to hear. Before the trip was over, he had put his faith in Jesus Christ. I look back to that and think, Wow! What could be better than being in Alaska on a hunting trip with the opportunity to fish for men!

In the 360° stewardship of relationships, the making of disciples is imperative. It is something we absolutely, positively must do. Jesus said emphatically, "Go...and make disciples of all nations..."[9] This statement is not a recommendation or a suggestion. It is a command of our Lord to His followers of all generations. And, according to John's Gospel, when we obey this command, we show that we are true disciples of Christ.[10] Disciple making is not synonymous with evangelism, but it begins with evangelism. First, a person is led to faith in Christ; then that person is led to follow Christ. Leading someone to faith in Christ is evangelism. Leading someone to follow Christ wholeheartedly is disciple making. The process of discipleship begins the instant a person trusts in Jesus as Lord and Savior, and it continues throughout a believer's life. To make a disciple is to guide a new or immature believer to spiritual maturity. It involves these essentials:

Leading someone to faith in Christ is evangelism. Leading someone to follow Christ wholeheartedly is disciple making.

Equipping them with the Word of God. To grow in Christ one must grow in the Word. Writing on this subject, Paul advised the Colossians, "Let the word of Christ dwell in you richly as you teach and admonish one another with all wisdom."[11] When he gave his final good-bye to the elders at Ephesus—men he had personally discipled—Paul said, "I have not hesitated to proclaim to you the whole will of God."[12] He had communicated to them a full and adequate understanding of God's Word and God's will. We have exactly the same priority in making disciples today—imparting the truths of Scripture to others so that they might mature in their faith.

Engaging them in sharing their faith. One of the most natural activities for a new believer is to share the life-transforming truth that he or she has discovered. This was the response of Andrew, one of the first disciples. The Bible says, "Andrew, Simon Peter's brother, was one of the two who heard what John had said and who had followed Jesus. The first thing Andrew did was to find his brother Simon and tell him, 'We have found the Messiah' (that is, the Christ). Then he brought Simon to Jesus."[13] Even as a brand-new, fledgling disciple, Andrew was already evangelizing, already sharing his faith. This is exactly as it should be. Courses and classes in personal evangelism are often helpful, but most important of all is that believers actually evangelize. There is no substitute for sharing one's faith, because each personal testimony is unique and powerful. When you tell how God has transformed your life, there is nothing anyone can say to disagree or refute your witness. That's how it

One of the most natural activities for a new believer is to share the life-transforming truth that he or she has discovered.

was for a blind man who was healed by Jesus. When he was called before the religious authorities he told them, "One thing I do know. I was blind but now I see!"[14] I urge you, use your influence to tell the story of your own spiritual journey and to engage others in doing likewise.

Encouraging them to steward their lives for the glory of God. When we understand that the purpose of life is to serve God and bring Him glory, it motivates us to encourage other believers—especially new believers—to invest their lives in fulfilling the same purpose. In Christ we have a newness of life that results in new ways of thinking, feeling, speaking and acting. His Spirit within us is the enabling power to break old habits and form new patterns of behavior. As we become more aware of His Word and more conscious of His will, we grow stronger in the faith. With the increase in our own spiritual maturity we can have increasing influence in the lives of other people. This leads us directly to the third objective.

Influencing People to Live a Normal Christian Life

If Jesus is your Savior and Lord, in all of your relationships—whether to family, friends, acquaintances or others—you are a witness for Him. By what you do and say, by how you act and react, by the attitudes you display, others will see Him either honored or dishonored. It is inevitable that, positively or negatively, you will affect the lives of other people. The most important concern then is how to ensure that your influence is positive. No one expects nor can anyone reach perfection; but we can attain balance, and this is central to making the most of your impact upon others. This was an essential idea set forth by

Watchman Nee, a leader of the church in China who died as a martyr for Christ in 1972. In his profoundly challenging way, Nee urged believers to live "a normal Christian life"—one that is spiritually whole and balanced. As he explained, balance implies the spiritual steadiness that comes from walking with Christ and running the race of faith. The balance that others observe in you is not physical steadiness but spiritual equilibrium, which is expressed in balanced thinking, emotions, speech and actions.

What they see in your life can inspire others to replicate in their own lives. Let's consider each of those four areas:

A "normal Christian life" is one that is spiritually whole and balanced, with a steadiness that comes from walking with Christ and running the race of faith.

Influencing how others think.

The well-balanced Christian thinks clearly and positively. Thinking clearly means maintaining the right view of God, of self and of life situations. This facilitates wise decision making and correct judgment about the big things in life as well as the small things. Thinking positively is a matter of looking for and finding the good even when everything may seem bad. It also means focusing on solutions as well as problems. Negative thinkers can have a damaging and even destructive effect upon those around them because negativity by its very nature pulls down rather than builds up. Exercising his influence with the Philippians, the apostle Paul gave them very specific instructions that we, too, should heed: "Finally, brothers, whatever is true, whatever is noble, whatever is right, whatever is pure, whatever is lovely, whatever is admirable—if anything is excellent or praiseworthy—think about such things."[15]

Influencing how others feel. Every person (including, of course, everyone within your sphere of influence) wants to feel appreciated and feel affirmed. This is true not just of Christians but also of every human being. The right use of influence can evoke these important feelings. By communicating healthy praise and honest gratitude to others, you magnify their sense of true worth. And when you communicate genuine acceptance and admiration, the other person feels affirmed. "Let your way of life be always seasoned with salt," says Colossians 4:6. Salt is a preservative that keeps things from spoiling—including relationships. As an influencer, live in a way that is loving and graceful, never corrupt. People are watching you, and your behavior has the potential to make them feel positive about Jesus Christ and be drawn to Him or to feel negative and be driven away from Him.

Influencing how others speak. "The tongue is a fire" says the book of James. The words we speak have tremendous power—the power to warm another person's heart or shatter it to pieces. They can hurt or heal. Words, in fact, can often hurt far more than deeds. Words of rejection can destroy a person's spirit, but words of encouragement can lift the spirit and make it soar. James 3:3-4 compares the influence of words to the way a horse is restrained by the bit and bridle and the way a ship is controlled by a small rudder. In the exercise of influence, what you say must be careful and constructive in order to promote the same kind of carefulness and constructiveness in the persons whom you influence.

Influencing how others act. The old adage says that actions speak louder than words, and this is true in the sense that actions are physically observed while words are mentally absorbed. Ideally, there should be no conflict between your actions and your words as you practice the stewardship of influence. When you act responsibly and wisely, those whom you influence can see your example and follow it. That was Paul's strategy in making disciples among the Corinthians when he told them to imitate his way of life. He wrote to them, "Follow my example, as I follow the example of Christ."[16] Paul wasn't asking them to be his disciples, but to be Christ's disciples in the same way that he was. Through his influence they would learn to act prudently and with true spiritual confidence.

Making an Impact

When I think of a truly influential Christian many people come to mind, but at the top of the list I would have to put William Tyndale. Though he lived hundreds of years ago, his life and his work affect us every day. In case you don't believe me, let me pose a couple of questions: Have you ever wondered where your English Bible came from? Have you ever been curious as to who was most instrumental in translating the ancient Scriptures into our modern English language? The answer to those important questions is discovered in one extraordinary man, William Tyndale. More than any other person in the past 500 years, Tyndale shaped not only our English Bible but our English language as well. Talk about influence!

William Tyndale was born in England sometime between 1490 and 1495. In 1510 he began his theological studies at Oxford. Eleven years later, in 1521, Tyndale was ordained to the priesthood and began preaching widely. In the first year of his public ministry, Tyndale spoke out against corruption within the Church and was accused of being a heretic. But he was most burdened by the fact that there was no Bible in the English language, so he resolved to translate the Scriptures.

When Tyndale made his solemn decision to put the words of the Bible into his own language, his fate was sealed. It was illegal to do such a thing in England. Under constant pressure and threats against his life, Tyndale journeyed to Germany to enlist the assistance of Martin Luther, who was then working on a translation of the Bible into German. With Luther's encouragement, Tyndale worked tirelessly to produce his first English edition of the New Testament. But his secret project was discovered and Tyndale was forced to flee to the city of Cologne. In that place as well he encountered opposition and the Senate of Cologne voted to prohibit him from printing and distributing his unlawful work.

More than any other person in the past 500 years, Tyndale shaped not only our English Bible but our English language as well. Talk about influence!

From Cologne, William Tyndale traveled to the city of Worms, where he completed the translation and printing of the first edition of the English New Testament in 1525. Brave messengers smuggled those historic new books into England, but nearly every copy was seized and burned. Of the 3,000 that were produced, only three remain, and only one of those is complete. The Archbishop of Canterbury, William Warham, took the extraordinary step of buying numerous copies before they reached England for the express purpose of burning them himself! When the news of Tyndale's scandalous translation was made public, a warrant was issued and the authorities in Worms attempted to arrest him. He escaped moments before they arrived.

On the run but always at work, Tyndale continued to translate the Scriptures. Friends and associates urged him to return to England, but Tyndale feared hostility from the ecclesiastical authorities and remained in Europe in order to finish his breakthrough work. In 1535, Tyndale was betrayed by a friend and was captured and imprisoned at Vilvorde Castle, the state prison near Brussels.

On October 6, 1536, William Tyndale was garroted and his body then burned at the stake. His last words were, "Lord, open the King of England's eyes."

Despite the appeals of influential English merchants and the royal adviser, Thomas Cromwell, Tyndale was tried and convicted of heresy. He was sentenced to die for his "crimes." Because he had offended Henry VIII, the king made no effort to intercede on Tyndale's behalf. On October 6, 1536, William Tyndale was garroted and his body then burned at the stake. His last words were, "Lord, open the King of England's eyes."

Though his greatest work was produced while he was in exile from his native land, Tyndale was the most influential figure of the English Reformation. His writings shaped the thought of the Puritans and his translation of the Bible essentially created the modern English language. Tyndale's work formed the basis of the famed Authorized Version, the King James Bible of 1611, which incorporated over 91% of his work. Literally thousands of the words and phrases which have become commonplace in the English language to this very day originated with Tyndale's translation of the Scriptures. It is often said that William Shakespeare's phraseology influenced the making of the King James Bible. Actually, the opposite is true, for it was Tyndale who first influenced Shakespeare. Scholars have now recorded over 5,000 instances in which William Shakespeare used the wording, syntax and phrasing of William Tyndale!

If someone asks where your Bible came from, don't say you got it at the Christian bookstore. Tell them that it came through the God-blessed work of a man who stewarded his influence in a way that made history—the father of our modern English language, the incomparable William Tyndale.

Stewarding Your Own Influence, Making Your Own Impact

As you steward your own influence in every relationship of life, let me encourage you to reflect on the apostle Paul's letter to the Philippians. Though only a few pages in length it has profound depth, filled with insights about the meaning of committed relationships. Paul was in jail when he wrote his deeply personal letter to the Christians at Philippi. Incarcerated in the dark isolation of a Roman prison, he could have been so depressed, but the great apostle had the encouraging influence of happy memories. He thought back to Philippi and his mind overflowed with joyous remembrances of what God had done in so many lives in that strategic city. In the first part of the first chapter, Paul shares something of what the memories meant to him. His heartfelt words instruct us in the ways we can steward our relationships with people in general and with our Christian brothers and sisters in particular.

Be thankful for people. Paul writes, "I thank my God every time I remember you."[17] Rather than feel sorry for himself (as many of us do when we're in dire circumstances), he thought of the Philippian Christians and thanked God for them. Actually, he had several reasons to scold them; but he set those things aside and gave thanks for all that was praiseworthy in them. Paul's thankfulness was directed to God, because He was the one who had made their relationship possible. His feelings were prompted by a heart full of loving gratitude.

- - -

Paul had several reasons to scold them; but he set those things aside and gave thanks for all that was praiseworthy.

- - -

Think of the people in your life—loved ones who are closest to you, extended family members, friends, acquaintances, classmates, co-workers, teammates, neighbors and others. God has blessed you with the opportunity to know each one, to learn from them, to share with them, to experience the ups and downs of life with them. Thank Him for those people with consistent appreciation.

Be thoughtful of people. Every time that Paul remembered his friends at Philippi, he was spiritually and emotionally joined with them once again.[18] Though physically separated by a great distance, he was with them in a very real way. For most of us, memories fade. Even some of the most sensitive relationships are all too soon forgotten: childhood friends...high school buddies...close neighbors...and often we can't even remember their names! Paul held the Philippians in his heart and mind and he simply would not let his memories fade. Some of the things that happened to Paul in Philippi could have produced sorrow—his illegal arrest, the beating he received, his discomfort in prison—but even those things brought joyous recollections of the relationships he had established.

Being thoughtful means putting the interests of others before your own interests, having the heart of a servant just as Jesus did. It means truly listening and truly caring in every way that is reasonably possible. And when you pray for others, be specific and focused, interceding just as Paul did for the Philippians whenever he was away from them.

Be trustworthy with people. The foundation of strong human relationships is trust. If there is no trust there can be no viable connection or communication. Marriages fall apart when trust is broken. Businesses crumble when partners violate their agreements. Wars are launched when nations go against the treaties they once signed. Trust is vital and trustworthiness is imperative at all levels of society. As Christians we have a unique understanding of this because trust is the basis of our relationship to God: we place our faith (our full trust) in the person and work of Christ. And, because we believe in Him and belong to Him, we have the potential of an even deeper relationship with one another as His children. Our "partnership in the Gospel,"[19] as Paul called it, transcends all kinds of barriers, enabling people from radically different backgrounds to share a spiritual bond that is indescribable. I have traveled around the world and visited dozens of nations, and wherever I have met fellow Christians I am profoundly conscious of the real meaning of "partnership in the Gospel." There is a connection, and there is communication; and it is very special.

To be trustworthy is to be one on whom others can depend. In the 360° stewardship of your relationships this is paramount. So, keep your promises, honor your word and do what is right. Relationships must be cultivated and maintained; they don't simply happen (even among Christians). Don't wait for others to take the initiative and then complain that people don't really care for you! Be proactive and be determined to make the most of every opportunity to connect with those whom God brings along the pathway of your life. Don't miss what He has in store for you.

Don't wait for others to take the initiative and then complain that people don't really care for you! Be proactive and be determined to make the most of every opportunity.

When I began to think about this subject of stewarding relationships, the first person who came to mind was Faye Gordon. I'm sure you have never heard of Faye because she isn't famous and she has never sought attention or acclaim. When I served as pastor of a rapidly growing church in Miami, Faye Gordon was the director of our nursery. On Easter Sunday one year, Faye came to me in tears and said, "Pastor, we are overwhelmed with babies! Please, please expand our facilities!" Of course, we responded to her emotional (but very reasonable) request, because everyone knew that she cared for those precious children as if they were her own. Since sometime in the 1950s she had faithfully served week after week, stewarding her commitment to the littlest people in our very large congregation.

Whether she was gently rocking a newborn, singing a song or quoting Bible verses to a cooing child, Faye Gordon showed a tenderness and care that still brings a smile to my face. She was also a great source of wisdom to first-time mothers, giving each one a feeling of much-needed confidence. In 1994, Faye retired from the nursery after nearly four decades of changing diapers and changing lives. Because of her faithfulness in stewarding her relationships, parents were able to hear the Gospel, couples were able to worship together, and thousands of children were blessed by the gentleness of an exceptional woman. On the day she retired, we had a special service, celebrating her life with roses and gifts and recognition. Without prompting, the entire church rose in a huge, sustained standing ovation. It was a fitting tribute to a lady whose Christ-like spirit showed all of us how devotion can make such a difference.

Counting on Accountability

The American statesman Daniel Webster was once asked, "What is the greatest thought you have ever contemplated?" He replied, "The greatest thought I have ever had and the most important thing I have ever learned is that I am personally accountable to the God of all Creation." According to Romans 14:12, each one of us must give an account of ourselves directly to God. It is difficult to even imagine what that moment will be like; but I am certain that it will happen, and I want Him to say, "Well done, good and faithful servant."[20] I agree with Webster that there is no thought more sobering, but I would add that there is no motivation more powerful than the fact that we will face the Lord and give an account of our lives.

I bring up this subject of accountability because it is a governing principle in the stewarding of our relationships with other people. As John Andrew Holmes quipped, "The entire population of the universe, with one little exception, is composed of others." That "one little exception" is you. You do not exist in a vacuum, and your success will not be achieved in isolation. God has placed you in a world of people to whom you must relate and to whom you are accountable. For example, God places spiritual leaders in positions of authority, and we are told in Scripture: "Obey your leaders and submit to their authority. They keep watch over you as men who must give an account. Obey them so that their work will be a joy, not a burden, for that would be of no advantage to you."[21] I find it so interesting in this verse that the accountability runs both ways: just as we are accountable to our spiritual leaders, they are accountable for us. As for the other relationships of life, the Bible says, "Let no debt remain outstanding, except the continuing debt to love one another, for he who loves his fellowman has fulfilled the law."[22]

The 360° stewarding of relationship demands personal fidelity, integrity and devotion. It is a responsibility to fulfill with joy—a heartfelt decision to please the Lord in word, deed and attitude of heart.

CHAPTER
FOUR
~ ~ ~ ~
# PRAYING WITH PURPOSE
Stewarding Every Concern

It would be impossible for me to overemphasize the importance of prayer. No spiritual activity is greater in significance or in consequence, or more relevant to the 360° stewardship of life. Every concern that touches us can be stewarded with prayer. I have no idea how many sermons I have preached and lessons I have taught on the subject of prayer, yet I am certain that I've barely scratched the surface! What a profound, mysterious thing prayer is: our personal means of communication with the One who spoke the worlds into existence. Where do we begin to explore this priceless spiritual privilege that God has given us? The answer that comes most readily to mind is to look first to Jesus. What did He say about prayer that can equip us for stewarding this vital commitment?

Luke 11:1 says, "One day Jesus was praying in a certain place. When he finished, one of his disciples said to him, 'Lord, teach us to pray, just as John taught his disciples.'" This disciple, whoever he was, had observed the prayer life of Jesus and he made one of the most important requests any believer can put before the Lord: Teach us to pray. What a wise request, because effectiveness in the Christian life is inseparably connected to one's effectiveness in prayer. Prayer is an absolute necessity: it is to the spiritual dimension what breathing is to the physical. And how long could you manage without breathing?

Fortunately, Jesus answered the disciple's request. In Matthew's Gospel we read a fuller account of what He said:

> "This, then, is how you should pray:
>
> 'Our Father in heaven, hallowed be your name,
>
> your kingdom come, your will be done
>
> on earth as it is in heaven.
>
> Give us today our daily bread.
>
> Forgive us our debts, as we also have forgiven our debtors.
>
> And lead us not into temptation, but deliver us from the evil one.'"[1]

The Disciple's Prayer

This is often called "the Lord's Prayer," although a more accurate term would be "the Disciple's Prayer" since it is a pattern intended to teach us how to pray in the will of God. It is a mistake to think of this prayer as something that must be constantly repeated, as if there is a certain blessing received each time you recite it. This prayer is a model for us to follow, not a form for us to recite. Constant repetition of a prayer can become an empty ritual—like some kind of rosary, minus the beads.

Pray to the Father. "Our Father" is such a rich, two-fold expression. As I read this phrase, the word "Our" reminds me of the relationship that I share with other Christians, and the word "Father" reminds me of my relationship to God. Notice that this model prayer contains no personal pronouns in the singular form. This is a family prayer, involving the Father in heaven and His children on earth. As members of this family we must want what the Father wants because His name is "hallowed"—it is holy and honored. Prayer, rightly so, starts with respect for the Father, not the requests of the Father's children. This is why it is so beneficial to begin a dedicated time of prayer with praise to God for who He is, our loving, gracious Father.

- - -

We are to pray that God's kingdom would come and that His will would be done. His desire must be our desire; and if it is any other way, we are the ones who need realignment.

- - -

Pray for God's kingdom to come and His will to be done. We are to pray that God's kingdom would come and that His will would be done. His desire must be our desire; and if it is any other way, we are the ones who need realignment. Anything in my praying that does not advance God's kingdom or glorify His name is against His will. We must not lose sight of the fact that Jesus came for one purpose only: to do the will of the Father. He reminded the disciples of this repeatedly because He wanted them to understand that it was their purpose as well—as it is for us as disciples today.

Pray for needs to be met. God's concerns take precedence over our concerns. As we grow in spiritual maturity and learn more of what it means to seek first the kingdom of God and His righteousness, our requests in prayer change. The Lord is concerned about the needs we have, but He wants us to see those needs in the context of higher purposes. Because He loves us, He will provide for us, meeting our needs day by day. In the Sermon on the Mount, Jesus said, "Ask and it will be given to you; seek, and you will find; knock and the door will be opened to you. For everyone who asks receives; he who seeks finds; and to him who knocks, the door will be opened."[2] Then

The Lord is concerned about the needs we have, but He wants us to see those needs in the context of higher purposes.

He concludes with an illustration and a phenomenal promise: "Which of you, if his son asks for bread, will give him a stone? Or if he asks for a fish, will give him a snake? If you, then, though you are evil, know how to give good gifts to your children, how much more will your Father in heaven give good gifts to those who ask him!"[3] From His eternal riches He will faithfully supply our "daily bread" and meet all of our needs.

Pray for forgiveness. To pray, "Forgive us our debts..." is similar to praying, "Forgive us our sins...." The word translated "debt" in many English versions refers to an obligation that has been incurred, either by a sin of omission or commission. For these obligations to be "forgiven" is for them to be cancelled. The emphasis in this part of the Disciple's Prayer is on the necessity of our forgiving one another. This verse is not referring to the forgiveness that leads to salvation, but the forgiveness that leads to harmony within the family of God. If we are not forgiving toward one another we cannot live in fellowship with one another or with the Lord. But, thankfully, as John wrote in his first epistle, "If we confess our sins, he is faithful and just and will forgive us our sins and purify us from all unrighteousness."[4]

Pray for deliverance. The concluding phrase of Christ's model prayer says, "And lead us not into temptation, but deliver us from the evil one." This temporal world in which we live is under the influence of Satan and his demonic agents. He is "the evil one" to whom this prayer refers, and it is from him that we pray to be delivered. As long as we live in this world we will be subjected to temptations and trials, but God will enable us to resist and withstand whatever comes against us. The battle in which we are engaged is a spiritual conflict, and His intervention gives us a spiritual deliverance. As Paul wrote to the Corinthians, "Though we live in the world, we do not wage war as the world does. The weapons we fight with are not the weapons of the world. On the contrary, they have divine power to demolish strongholds."[5]

Prayer is a great privilege that demands a deep commitment, a commitment that must be stewarded with wisdom and care. I urge you: Pray unceasingly, pray expectantly and pray earnestly. As James 5:16 reminds us, the prayer of a righteous person "is powerful and effective."[6]

One of the most beautiful, loving things we can do for other people is to pray for them. When we do, the result is always meaningful and sometimes miraculous. A prayer is a gift in the truest sense, because the blessing and benefit is focused on the recipient, not the giver. For the Christian, this kind of prayer is a vital element of one's spiritual life. In technical terms, it's called intercession—the act of pleading for the sake of another person, making an appeal on their behalf. Intercession stands in contrast to the other forms of prayer we practice, most of which are centered on our own relationship to God. Petition, for example, is prayer that asks God for His provision. Confession is prayer in which we confess our sins and failings to God. Adoration is prayerful worship, expressing praise for God's goodness and greatness, honoring Him simply for who He is. Thanksgiving is, clearly, giving thanks to God for His faithful supply of all we need, His gifts both seen and unseen.

When we give the gift of intercessory prayer, we invite the power of God to act in another person's life. In doing so, we too are blessed.

Intercession is prayer that moves us out of the realm of personal interest and into specific concerns for specific people. When we give the gift of intercessory prayer, we invite the power of God to act in another person's life. In doing so, we too are blessed. As we intercede, He intervenes; and His intervention can come through material provision, spiritual enablement, and emotional or physical healing. "Pray for each other," James wrote in his epistle, "so that you may be healed."[7]

Christians often glibly say to one another, "I'll be praying for you" without ever getting around to actually praying. I know this to be the case because I've done it so often myself! I need this reminder as much as anyone because I'm so prone to good intentions that never make it to the point of actual implementation. Admittedly, I'm admonishing myself as much in this chapter as I'm admonishing you! This is a truly important commitment, a practice that was perfectly modeled by Jesus Christ.

The True Lord's Prayer

As we've already seen, what we commonly call "The Lord's Prayer" is actually not the Lord's Prayer at all, but a sample prayer that Jesus gave to His disciples. The true Lord's Prayer is found in chapter 17 of John's Gospel, which is devoted entirely to the prayer of intercession Jesus prayed for His followers. By examining what He prayed for us, we can discover how to intercede for others, how to give the gift of prayer for their blessing and benefit. Let's take a closer look at a few choice words in the true "Lord's prayer" in John 17...

> "Now this is eternal life: that they may know you, the only true God, and Jesus Christ, whom you have sent." [8]

Pray that others may know God. Nothing in this temporal, earthly life is more important than knowing the key to the next life—the eternal, heavenly life to come. That key is knowledge—knowledge of "the only true God" and the one whom He sent, His Son Jesus Christ. This is not "head" knowledge we're talking about. It runs much deeper than merely knowing about God intellectually. One must also know Him experientially, personally committing to Him in a relationship of faith and fidelity.

As we pray for others to know God, these truths guide our intercession. Christian moms and dads, for example, intercede for their children, praying that their sons and daughters will not only know *about* God, but truly *know* God. Christian bosses intercede for their employees; Christian employees intercede for their bosses as well as their colleagues, praying that those with whom they work will know God in truth. Caring Christians in all of life's relationships realize that the 360° stewardship of concern for others leads us inevitably to prayer on their behalf.

> "Holy Father, protect them by the power of your name..." [9]

> "My prayer is not that you take them out of the world but that you protect them from the evil one." [10]

Pray that others may be protected by God. This is a troubled, turbulent, world. It doesn't take even 60 seconds reading the headlines in the local paper or on the internet to realize that there are threats to our well-being and our security. Since 9/11 the risks have become such a concern that we now have a color scheme to indicate perceived levels of danger.

To a certain extent, governmental agencies and military forces can protect us, but the only reliable protection comes from another authority: God Himself. Only in Him are we truly secure; only He can provide genuine protection. And when Jesus prayed in His intercessory prayer, "Holy Father, protect them by the power of your name," He was referring to something deeper than physical protection. His plea is for the spiritual protection of believers in a world that is adamantly opposed to Christ and to all who follow Him.

From what do we need to be spiritually protected? I can suggest several things: We need protection from the lure of this world's wealth. We need protection from the pull of pride. And we certainly need protection from the pursuit of pleasure. Materialism, pride and sinful pleasure are like magnets, forcefully attracting us to their sphere. That force can only be countered by another, stronger force—the power of God's name. God's desire is that we be in the world, but not of it; and while we are in it, to live with an "other-worldly" mindset. Wouldn't you love to know that people are praying for you in this way? What a gift this is to one another!

- - -

The only reliable protection comes from God Himself. Only in Him are we truly secure; only He can provide genuine protection.

- - -

> "I say these things...so that they may have the full measure of my joy within them." [11]

Pray that others will have true joy. Everyone wants to be happy. We're so focused on happiness as a society that we will do just about anything to get it. But happiness is completely relative to one's circumstances. If I'm faced with health problems, if I've just lost my job, if I don't have enough set aside for retirement, if, if, if... then it's likely I won't be happy. But joy is entirely different. Things can be going very badly, yet as a follower of Christ I can still have a heart full of joy in the bad times as well as the good times.

One of the classics of Christian literature—still in print today—is a multi-volume set called Foxe's *Book of Martyrs*. Written by John Foxe in the 1600s, the *Book of Martyrs* recounts the experiences of men and women who literally gave their lives in service to Jesus Christ. Their physical lives were ended with gruesome brutality; yet in so many of the accounts, they are reported as having died with a smile on the face, words of forgiveness for their tormenters on their lips, even with laughter at the moment of death. In the face of unspeakable evil, they had joy! They weren't crazy or deluded in any way; their joy was deep and genuine because God had given it to them.

As you intercede for others, pray that they will have the "full measure" of Christ's joy, no matter what their circumstances may be.

As you intercede for others, pray that they will have the "full measure" of Christ's joy, no matter what their circumstances may be. Pray that they will experience the settled satisfaction that He alone can give. Pray that their desire would not be just for happiness, but for the joy that transcends every personal struggle, every difficulty, every trial.

"Sanctify them by the truth; your word is truth." [12]

Pray that others will be spiritually dedicated. *Sanctify* is an old word that has a special significance. It means "to set apart for God"—to be spiritually dedicated. When Jesus prayed that His followers would be sanctified by the truth, He was wanting them to know and obey the Word of God.

When you pray for others—whether they are family, friends, neighbors, pastors, teachers, fellow church members or even strangers—pray like Jesus prayed. Ask God to sanctify them by the truth. In other words, ask Him to use the truths of Scripture to purify and prepare their lives for effective Christian service. So often in my experience as a pastor and Christian leader I have been guided by a particular truth of the Bible, sometimes just a word or phrase, only to learn later that someone was praying that Scripture into my life. My life was enriched because someone was praying to God on my behalf. That is humbling and challenging.

Never underestimate the importance of the time you spend praying for the spiritual dedication of another person.

> "My prayer is not for them alone. I pray also for those who will believe in me through their message..." [13]

Pray that others will be spiritually fruitful. Jesus was not praying only for His original followers. His intercession was "also for those who will believe in me through their message...." In that one important statement He enfolded every believer of every era since the moment of His return to heaven. That means He was praying for you and me! And just as those first followers were to be faithful in spreading the message of Christ, so are we to faithfully tell the Good News to our generation. The objective of the message we deliver is "that the world may believe" in Jesus Christ.

God's plan is to communicate His message through human

beings. Prone as we are to stumbles and failings, we're still His chosen vessels, His messengers of grace. And for that we desperately need to pray for one another. Nothing is more spiritually invigorating than telling the message of Christ's love and salvation. But for some reason, nothing is more intimidating to so many Christians. Pray that those in the circle of your life who know Jesus Christ will be empowered and emboldened to share their faith. Pray that they will be effective messengers, clearly expressing the reason for their hope.

> "May they be brought to complete unity to
> let the world know that you sent me and have
> loved them even as you have loved me." [14]

Pray that we will all experience true unity in Christ. The golden thread woven through the words of Jesus' prayer in John 17 is spiritual unity. Just as Jesus and the Father are one, He prayed that His followers would also be one—united in spirit and purpose to do His will.

In unity there is strength, infinitely greater strength than we could ever experience independently. As we think of one another and pray for one another, may we never forget that we are united with God in Christ, and because of that union we have access to the Father. We may go to different churches, work in different ministries or have differing views on some doctrines, but all who have been born of the Spirit are members of one body, one family. We belong to one another in the most profound relationship, and that's why Paul urges us to "keep the unity of the Spirit through the bond of peace." [15]

The door is open for us to go through at any time, in any circumstance of life, communicating directly with the One who spoke the worlds into existence. He invites us to come with all our concerns and to steward them in conversation with Him. When we come we do so with adoration, with confession, with petition, with thanksgiving, and—very importantly—with intercession for one another.

CHAPTER
FIVE
~~~~
WHAT'S IN YOUR HAND?
Stewarding Every Ability

Sometimes I read the Bible and catch myself laughing out loud. Almost always, I'm chuckling because I see myself in the frailties and failures of people described in various stories of the Scriptures. It happened just the other day when I was reading the familiar account of God's call to Moses. I think we often imagine Moses as actually looking and acting like Charlton Heston in *The Ten Commandments*. But, of course, he was probably nothing at all like that. And his reactions to the call of God are hardly that of a hero. The Lord had appeared to Moses very dramatically, drawing his attention to a bush that burned but was not consumed by the flames. God then spoke to Moses and told him of the bold mission on which he was to embark. His response was to immediately begin asking questions and making excuses. *Who am I to do this? What would I say?* Who would believe me? And to each doubting question, God would give the reassurance of His enabling power. Finally, Moses asks one question too many and God gives him an object lesson. Let's read the incident as the Bible describes it in the first verses of Exodus, chapter 4...

Moses answered, "What if they do not believe me or listen to me and say, 'The LORD did not appear to you'?"

Then the LORD said to him, "What is that in your hand?"

"A staff," he replied.

The LORD said, "Throw it on the ground."

Moses threw it on the ground and it became a snake, and he ran from it.

Then the LORD said to him, "Reach out your hand and take it by the tail."

So Moses reached out and took hold of the snake and it turned back into a staff in his hand.

"This," said the LORD, "is so that they may believe that the LORD, the God of their fathers—the God of Abraham, the God of Isaac and the God of Jacob—has appeared to you." [1]

The Defining Question

Notice the question that God asks Moses: *"What is that in your hand?"* No other question could be more relevant to our own lives, because God wants to take whatever we have and turn it into an instrument of His power. He wants to perform a miracle of transformation in order to use us in His service in an extraordinary way. Like Moses, we may have become too accustomed to the day-in, day-out regularity of life; and God sometimes decides to upset our routines. In Moses' case, his life had already been divided into two eras: as a prince in Egypt from birth to age 40, and as a shepherd in the desert from age 40 to 80. Moses had fled from Egypt, running for his life after a misguided, murderous attempt to identify with his own people, the Jews. In the remote loneliness of the desert he had brooded over that failure for four long decades. He was undoubtedly gripped with a feeling of hopelessness about the Hebrew nation—who were not really a nation so much as an unorganized mob of slaves in Egypt. Then, it happened: God suddenly intervened and called Moses to the high adventure of service.

After all of the Lord's promises, Moses was still reluctant to commit. At that point, God asked, "What is that in your hand?

As we know, Moses did not react with excitement and eagerness to meet the challenge. To the contrary, he was dismayed and instantly overcome with doubts about himself and about how the Hebrew people would react to his intervention. Understandably, he felt inadequate for the mission and unfit for the task. He tried to get out of it, but God replied with amazing assurances that He would be with him, that the people would believe him, and even that the Egyptians would be favorably disposed toward Moses and the Israelites. Yet, after all of the Lord's promises, Moses was still reluctant to commit. At that point, God asked, "What is that your hand?"

Significance in the Insignificant

The staff that Moses held in his hand was the tool of his trade as a shepherd. It represented who he was—an ordinary man with ordinary equipment. When Moses threw down the staff it became a snake; and when he picked it up it again became a wooden rod. There was nothing in the staff, nor in the life experience it stood for, to equip Moses in any way for the job of leading an entire nation out of bondage. And yet God wanted to use that shepherd's staff to make a vital point: God's will is to use the weak things to confound the mighty, to transform an object of little value into an awesome weapon that can break down the walls of opposition. It seems so insignificant, yet God wanted Moses to surrender his staff, to give it up and see what it really was—a symbol of the sinister, snake-like tendencies within his own heart and the complete inadequacy of his own abilities and resources.

The staff, symbolic of Moses' life, had been surrendered for God's use and had become an instrument of spiritual authority.

When the wooden staff became a snake, Moses ran from it. I doubt that any of us have ever seen an 80-year-old man move so quickly! But God called him back, and told Moses to pick up the slithering, dangerous snake by the tail. By faith (and I'm sure it took a lot of faith), he did what God told him to do; and the snake instantly became a rod in his hand once again. But this time, something was different. The staff, symbolic of Moses' life, had been surrendered for God's use and had become an instrument of spiritual authority. From that day forward, Moses increasingly realized that the simple wooden stick in his hand was representative of an infinite power—a power that would capture the attention of millions of people. Having grown up in Pharaoh's palace, Moses was not naive about the confrontation that lay ahead. He knew that the Egyptian king would be resistant and that the Israelite slaves would be frightened by the prospect of a revolt against their oppressors. But Moses knew that he was in the hand of God, as surely as the rod was in his own hand.

As we read further in the book of Exodus we discover that the staff is thereafter referred to as "the rod of God." In essence it no longer belongs to Moses because it has been surrendered to the Lord and is endued with His strength. It is the rod in Moses' hand when God brings judgment upon Egypt in the ten plagues. It is the rod lifted high as God splits the waters of the Red Sea. It is the rod which strikes the rock at Horeb, bringing streams of water from a boulder. In every instance, "the rod of God" is used to demonstrate His power and provision. And, tragically, it was the self-willed use of the rod which resulted in the greatest disappointment of Moses' life—a solemn reminder to us against using for selfish purposes anything that has been consecrated to God.

Who God Chooses and Who He Uses

The practice of 360° stewardship requires us to face the same question that God asked Moses: "What is that in your hand?" There is an innate tendency to think that only those persons who have remarkable skills and brilliant minds are the truly useful in God's service. But this question rebukes that idea. It is wrong to think that you could serve God more effectively if only you were more articulate, more intelligent or more gifted than someone else. The fact is that God loves you and wants you just as you are; yet He sees in you not what you are, but what you can be in His hand. Look at the group Jesus called to be His disciples—a rag-tag bunch of fishermen, a wild-eyed zealot, a despised tax collector and a few other less-than-desirable members of society. But that motley crew was used by Him to "turn the world upside down,"[2] according to the book of Acts. No person is more useful in the Lord's service than any other person who is equally obedient and yielded to God. The true measure of value is not one's prominence, superiority or popularity, but one's faith in God and commitment to Him. What we may view humanly as limitations or disabilities count for nothing in God's economy. This is a highly personal matter: God is asking what is in *your* hand.

Joni Eareckson was a vivacious teenager on a family vacation when she dove into shallow waters and struck her head on a rock. In one horrific instant she was left a quadriplegic for life, permanently disabled from the neck down. Through years of physical therapy and seemingly endless medical procedures, Joni endured a personal tribulation that few of us can fathom. According to her autobiography there were times that she despaired over not being able to take her own life, frustrated that her unresponsive limbs kept her from ending it all. But God pierced the darkness of Joni's despair with the floodlight of His grace. Through the witness of loving friends—who saw her as a person, not a victim—Joni came to faith in Jesus Christ. Putting her trust fully in the Lord, she yielded her life for Christian service. In spite of all her physical liabilities and limitations, Joni was ready and willing to be used by God. To her, stewarding every ability meant something transcendent.

More than 30 years have passed since Joni Eareckson Tada committed her life to Christ, and to say that she has been remarkably used by God since that day is quite an understatement. She is a bestselling author, an acclaimed artist and an internationally renowned speaker. Her life story was the subject of a widely distributed motion picture. Her works of art—done entirely by mouth with a paintbrush clinched in her teeth—have inspired countless people the world over. But Joni's greatest influence is through the organization that bears her name, Joni & Friends, which ministers to handicapped persons in dozens of countries, providing support programs, resources and thousands of wheelchairs. This "disabled" woman has turned out to be one of most able and effective persons of a generation, a shining example of a life fully devoted to Christ.

This "disabled" woman has turned out to be one of most able and effective persons of a generation, a shining example of a life fully devoted to Christ.

Answering God's Question

When we consider God's question to us—"What is that in your hand?"—we must realize that He isn't necessarily referring to something literal. Unlike Moses, we don't always carry around the tools of our trade or our identity. However, what we do have in common with Moses is this: In the same way that God called upon Moses to give everything he had, He calls upon you and me to do the same. He wants us to willingly offer ourselves in His service and for His purpose. Joni Eareckson understood this; and though she literally could not hold a staff in her hand, her yielded life has become a "rod of God" raised in spiritual triumph. The fact is, what any one of us actually has to offer to God is inconsequential. We are finite and He is infinite. But through His miraculous empowerment we are able to do His will on earth.

The stewarding of every ability has an entirely unique meaning to each of us. You are unique, your circumstances are unique.

So, again we face the question: What is that in your hand?

The stewarding of every ability has an entirely unique meaning to each of us. You are unique, your circumstances are unique, and you should appreciate your distinctiveness in God's plan. Please don't misconstrue the meaning of these statements. It is not my intention to encourage a self-centered mindset (which much of today's motivational literature does). To the contrary, think about yourself without thinking selfishly. In other words, always remember who you are and why you are here. You are a human being, created by a loving God, designed in His image and destined for His purposes. You are special in His eyes, and you have a role to play in His eternal plan. In fulfilling that unique role, 360° stewardship is imperative. Every blessing and benefit in your life is a factor in the stewardship equation. Your spiritual gifts, your natural abilities, your acquired skills, your material resources, your personal desires—all these and more are line items on the balance sheet of your life. How you manage these God-given resources determines your success as a steward.

When it comes to stewarding every ability, there are two essential topics: Your Spiritual Gifts and Your Spiritual Calling. Let's briefly explore each one.

Stewarding Your Spiritual Gifts

As a loving Father, God gives spiritual gifts to every one of His children. Simply stated, a spiritual gift is a Spirit-endowed ability for Christian service. It is purely an expression of grace, as indicated by the very word used in Scripture: our English word *gift* is from the Greek term *charisma*, which is derived from *charis*, the Greek word for grace. Two compelling passages of the New Testament, Romans 12:6-8 and 1 Corinthians 12:8-10, describe spiritual gifts and explain their purpose. When Christians are taught to identify their spiritual gifts and encouraged to exercise those gifts within a body of believers, then the church will function normally.

A spiritual gift is not a talent. Non-Christians have talents as well as Christians, but only Christians are spiritually gifted. Talents derive from natural ability, but spiritual gifts are the result of spiritual endowment. Talents instruct, inspire or entertain on a natural level; but gifts are for building up other believers or reaching out to unbelievers. Something supernatural occurs when a spiritual gift is exercised. Nothing supernatural occurs when a talent is used. Talents and gifts do have a relationship, but they are not one and the same.

Many years ago one of my mentors gave me an easy-to-remember list to help in identifying and using spiritual gifts. He called it his "ABCDE" method, with 5 key words to remember:

Awareness. Study God's Word and know what it says on the subject of spiritual gifts.

Belief. Trust in the promise that God has given you spiritual gifts to be used in His service. By grace, He gives the gifts; by faith, you put them into practice.

Confirmation. Prayerfully seek God's direction, asking Him to confirm the identity and reality of your spiritual gifts. Be aware that He will often use other Christians to reinforce your sense of confirmation.

Discernment. Don't confuse natural talents with spiritual gifts, but discern that one can be employed in the exercise of the other.

Exercise. Put your spiritual gifts into practice. Exercise them at every opportunity that God brings your way.

Throughout this process, ask meaningful questions: What do I seem equipped to do? What opportunity is at hand that I'm in a position to respond to? What are my deepest spiritual desires? How do I fit in with the other members of this body of believers? What are the needs that I am most moved to meet? Do others (especially spiritual leaders) recognize my gift(s) and appreciate my involvement? The answers to these questions can shed light and give a better understanding of your function within the Body of Christ.

Stewarding Your Spiritual Calling

Romans 11:29 states this monumental truth: "For God's gifts and his call are irrevocable." When God endows you with His gifts and extends His call to your life, He doesn't later change His mind and retract what He has given. As James says, "Every good and perfect gift is from above, coming down from the Father of the heavenly lights, who does not change like shifting shadows."[3] The first and foremost of His gifts is, of course, the gift of the new birth, granting us eternal life through His Son. "He chose to give us birth through the word of truth, that we might be a kind of firstfruits of all he created."[4] Our first calling, then, is a calling to salvation—to believe and receive Jesus Christ as Savior and Lord. By His Holy Spirit, God calls us to Himself and gives us His life. When we respond in faith, He then calls us to a life of Christ-centered service.

> *When God endows you with His gifts and extends His call to your life, He doesn't later change His mind and retract what He has given.*

Since the Bible is filled with stories of God's call to service, it is very difficult to single out a particular example. We could examine God's call to Abraham, directing him to leave his homeland and journey by faith to an unnamed land. We could explore the fascinating experience of Gideon, who struggled against doubts to follow God's directives. We could study the extraordinary story of Esther, who was called by God to literally save her people from annihilation. We could delve deep into the life of Paul, called to service as he lay blinded in the dust of a Damascan road. Any of these individuals could teach us so much about the stewardship of one's calling, but the person from whom I have learned the most on this subject is the apostle Peter. Perhaps it's because I can identify so readily with his bull-in-the-china-shop impulsiveness or his highly emotive relationship to Jesus. Whatever it is, his life speaks to me and he has taught me some priceless lessons in 360° stewardship.

Peter was one of the first two men called by Jesus to be His disciples. He and his brother, Andrew, left their fishing nets and followed the man they knew to be the Messiah. Peter was an eyewitness of the Lord's ministry, and with James and John was a member of the "inner circle" of the Twelve. After the resurrection of Christ and His ascension to heaven, Peter and the other disciples waited and prayed until the Holy Spirit came upon them. On the day of Pentecost, the promised power came, and they began to proclaim the Good News. Peter was the central character in the drama that unfolded, preaching the first sermon of a new era. The Book of Acts describes that amazing experience, and it gives us several key factors in following the call of God. Let's take a closer look at some of those factors...

Peter and John were uneducated, untrained men; yet they caused the highest-ranking religious leaders to marvel at them.

Spiritual Confidence. The Bible says that one day after Pentecost Peter and John were going up to the temple at the time of prayer when they were confronted by a beggar who had been crippled since birth. He asked them for money, but they gave him something far better: "Then Peter said, 'Silver or gold I do not have, but what I have I give you. In the name of Jesus Christ of Nazareth, walk.' Taking him by the right hand, he helped him up, and instantly the man's feet and ankles became strong. He jumped to his feet and began to walk."[5] A crowd quickly gathered to see this miraculous thing, and Peter seized the opportunity to preach the Gospel. For their outrageous "crime," the religious authorities threw Peter and John in jail for the night.

On the next day, when Peter and John were called before the ruling council, Peter once again began to preach. The Bible says that he was filled with the Spirit as he boldly declared the name and power of Christ and unashamedly proclaimed Jesus as the only way. He said to them, "Salvation is found in no one else, for there is no other name under heaven given to men by which we must be saved."[6] His words were startling to religious rulers who were not used to such blatant preaching. They were dumbstruck by the boldness of Peter and John.

Peter and his fellow disciple John were uneducated, untrained men. They were simple fishermen, coarse and unsophisticated. I wouldn't be surprised if people of that day told "fisherman" jokes! There wasn't anything exceptional about them, yet they caused the highest-ranking religious leaders to marvel at them. Just a few weeks before, however, Peter had denied that he even knew Jesus. What happened to cause such an astonishing change? Actually, several things had happened: Jesus had died, He had risen from the dead, He had ascended back to heaven, and the Holy Spirit had come as promised and empowered Christ's followers. Peter, along with the other disciples, was an eyewitness and a participant in these history-making events. He had been changed— indeed, he was still being changed—conformed to the character of Christ by the power of the Holy Spirit. As for the council, Acts 4:13 says, "When they saw the courage of Peter and John and realized that they were unschooled, ordinary men, they were astonished and they took note that these men had been with Jesus."

As you steward God's calling in your life, an essential element is spiritual confidence. Natural, human logic (and nearly all self-help books) say to believe in yourself, to follow your instincts, to confide in your abilities and intelligence. But I can tell you that true satisfaction and success come through believing in God and confiding in the Spirit's power—just like Peter learned to do.

Spiritual Conformity. Spiritual confidence must always be coupled with spiritual conformity—that is, conformity to Christ. In the 360° stewardship of your calling, ask yourself on a consistent basis: Am I becoming more like Christ? Is my life reflecting more of His character? You see, the evidence of a changed life is incontrovertible and it often leaves the skeptics speechless. That's what happened in this incident with Peter and John: "But since they could see the man who had been healed standing there with them, there was nothing they could say."[7] There sat that august body of religious leaders. Their faces were stern, their eyes firing daggers of hate at Peter and John. But their tongues were frozen. They could say nothing against what had happened. A man paralyzed for life had been healed. A good deed had been done. Yet they refused to acknowledge the overwhelming evidence of God's working. They admitted that a miracle had been done, but refused to admit that God had done it. They were "religious" but unbelieving, diametrically opposed to Christ and His followers—just like it is today in nations around the world.

The council warned Peter and John not to speak or teach in the name of Jesus. Blinded by pride and arrogance, they simply didn't want to hear any more of this. But the disciples were ready to give an answer: "Judge for yourselves whether it is right in God's sight to obey you rather than God."[8] The matter was so clear and convincing that all the authorities could have honestly said was, "Obey God rather than us." But they didn't. Instead, they threatened and blustered. Their hope was to maintain control by the threat of force, but it was simply not going to work. Peter and John chose to follow Christ, to conform to His will and to confide in the Spirit's power. They boldly replied: "For we cannot help speaking about what we have seen and heard."[9]

Peter and John chose to follow Christ, conform to His will and confide in the Spirit's power. They boldly replied: "For we cannot help speaking about what we have seen and heard."

Spiritual Conviction. The third element in the stewardship of God's calling is an unbending spiritual conviction about who God is, who you are and what your reason for being is. You acknowledge that God is your loving Father who saves you through His Son and empowers you by His Spirit. You realize that you are, as Paul said, "chosen...according to the plan of him who works out everything in conformity with the purpose of his will."[10] And you agree that the purpose of your life is to honor your Lord by communicating His truth, demonstrating His character and seeking His pleasure. Your all-encompassing reason to get up every morning is to seize the day for God's glory.

Making the most of all that you have and all that you are doesn't come down to you. It comes down to "Christ in you, the hope of glory."[11] Thankfully, the 360° stewardship of life is not an endless list of chores but an ever-increasing abundance of God's blessing on the one who seeks Him earnestly, loves Him wholeheartedly and follows Him unreservedly.

Thankfully, the 360° stewardship of life is not an endless list of chores but an ever-increasing abundance of blessings..

On Thursday, July 8, 2004, at 6:45 in the morning, my mom passed from this life into eternity with her Lord. For nearly all of her adult life she had lived for the Lord, for my dad and for her family. For the last 31 of those years she struggled against the constant downward pull of Parkinson's disease, never once complaining or being concerned for her own needs. Those final few days with her are vivid in my mind. Mom and Dad had been married for 50 years and three months, and as I watched my dad sit by her side during those waning hours, I could see more than ever how they were truly one. They never had much in the ways that the world measures worth, but they were rich in more important ways.

It had been my privilege to have them live with us the last nine years of Mom's life. On their 50th wedding anniversary we surprised them with a great number family and friends, and one of my dad's best friends said to me, "I will never forget when your dad and I traveled home from the Korean War for the wedding. When I looked at your mom I knew she loved him completely." How right he was. The years they were together, and especially the last hours they shared, made me realize what Mom loved about Dad. She loved his character, his faithfulness to her, his work ethic, his love for his boys, his commitment to church on Sundays, his dependability in always bringing his paycheck home to her. Those qualities in the end are all that matter anyway. In her last talk with me the Sunday before her "homegoing," she said, "Kirk, I have loved you for all of your life...you take care of my family for me now."

My wife, Denise, was holding my mom's hand on that bright Thursday morning, singing the old hymn *It is Well with My Soul* when Mom stepped into the presence of God. Denise said, "I loved your mother like she was my own. That God chose me to be sitting with her holding her hand when He called her home was my greatest honor in life. Peggy was the most like Jesus of any person I have ever known." It was my wife's birthday and she said, "This is God's present to me."

Just like my mom had done for so long, Denise was there, sitting in the chair of responsibility, meeting a challenge, stewarding a precious opportunity, using her God-given abilities and gaining a priceless blessing in the process.

For me, that moment said so much about 360° stewardship. It's about love, devotion, diligence and all the other things touched upon in this book. But, above all, it's about faithfulness. "So then, men ought to regard us as servants of Christ and as those entrusted with the secret things of God. Now it is required that those who have been given a trust must prove faithful."[12]

Envision a tennis racquet...a golf club...a football...a baseball...a guitar...a piano. On their own these are just inanimate objects. But...a tennis racquet in Venus Williams' hand...a golf club in Tiger Woods' hands...a football in Peyton Manning's hand...a baseball in Roger Clemens' hand...a guitar in Eric Clapton's hands...a piano played by Norah Jones' hands...all these inanimate objects come alive with meaning. If that is true of human hands, imagine the transformation of your life in God's hands.

CHAPTER
SIX

~ ~ ~ ~

MORE THAN MONEY
Stewarding Every Asset

At 12:55 p.m. the mayday call crackled through the speakers at the Flight Service Station on Alaska's Kenai Peninsula. The desperate pilot of a Piper A22, a small single-engine plane, was reporting that he had run out of fuel and was preparing to ditch the aircraft in the waters of Cook Inlet. On board were four people, two adults and two girls, ages 11 and 12. They had departed two hours earlier from Port Alsworth, a small community on the south shore of Lake Clark, bound for Soldotna, a distance of about 150 miles. Under normal conditions it would have been a routine flight; however, the combination of fierce headwinds and a failure to top off the fuel tank had created a lethal situation. Upon hearing the plane's tail number, the air traffic controller realized that his own daughter was one of the young passengers aboard the plane. In desperation himself, he did everything possible to assist the pilot; but suddenly the transmission was cut off. The plane had crashed into the icy waters.

Four helicopters operating nearby began searching the area within minutes of the emergency call; but they found no evidence of the plane, and no survivors. The aircraft had been traveling without water survival gear, leaving its four passengers with even less of a chance to make it through the ordeal. Fiercely cold Cook Inlet, with its unpredictable glacial currents, is considered among the most dangerous waters in the world. It can claim a life in minutes, and that day it claimed four.

For reasons we will never know, the pilot of that doomed aircraft chose not to use the assets that were at his disposal. He did not have enough fuel. He did not have the proper survival equipment. Perhaps he had not taken the time to get the day's weather report. Whatever the case, he failed to steward all the resources that were available; and in this instance the consequences were fatal.

This is a tragic story and my purpose in telling it is to emphasize that the 360° stewardship of assets is a serious business; and God's will is that we give it serious attention. This demands, first of all, that we recognize our assets and that we have the right perspective toward them. That is possible, of course, only if we have the right focus on our source. Let's be clear on that point: Everything that we have—every earthly asset both tangible and intangible—comes from a heavenly source. God is our faithful provider; and His plan is that we be His faithful stewards.

Taking Inventory of Your Assets

The resources entrusted to us by God are to be stewarded wisely and purposefully. Our tangible assets fall into two basic categories: monetary and material. Monetary resources include your income and all the funds that you have in your bank accounts, savings accounts and redeemable investments. Material resources include all the things that have potential value in terms of Christian stewardship: your home, your vehicles, and other earthly goods.

All assets, whether monetary or material, are the result of God's favor and blessing, not one's personal achievements. Therefore, the purpose in taking an inventory of these things is to quantify His blessings and consciously dedicate those assets to Him. In doing this we express to the Lord an attitude of stewardship versus one of ownership. "Our" resources actually belong to Him; but He gives us the privilege of using them, enjoying them and managing them for His glory.

Everything that we have—every earthly asset both tangible and intangible—comes from a heavenly source.

Investment Strategies that Lead to True Success

The God-given monetary and material assets in your life are to be invested in a way that brings the greatest return in spiritual terms. In God's economy, things are different from any worldly system of financial management or assessment; and it is essential that we understand His principles and follow His plan.

How to use your money. Regardless of the amount of money you have, it can be stewarded in a wise and spiritually profitable manner. To put it as simply as possible, there are three things to do with your money:

1. Give it willingly to accomplish God-honoring purposes.

2. Spend it reasonably to meet personal needs and fulfill personal desires.

3. Save it strategically in order to extend value and to keep meeting needs in the future.

Concerning the first of these priorities—giving purposefully to the Lord's work—I have written other books that examine the entire range of biblical principles governing how we live and how we give. This is a subject I dealt with every day for more than a decade, advising pastors and church leaders across America, helping them to realize their God-given vision for ministry. The ongoing needs of a church's ministry are met through ordinary giving—ordinary in the sense of being regular and consistent. However, extraordinary needs must be met with extraordinary giving—above and beyond all normal commitments. My personal conviction is that the giving of the tithe isn't an option but a responsibility, and when I give it I am expressing faithful obedience. Then, when I respond with an extraordinary gift to meet an extraordinary need, I am expressing faithful confidence. In both kinds of giving, I have a sense of duty but also a great sense of delight, knowing that I am honoring the Lord and partnering in His name.

When I give [the tithe] I am expressing faithful obedience. When I respond with an extraordinary gift to meet an extraordinary need, I am expressing faithful confidence.

In financial terms, some of us have been blessed with a lot and some with very little, but we can all give generously, joyously and sacrificially. God's measurement is in proportion to what we have been given: to whom much is given, much is required, Jesus said.[1] I have seen some very large financial gifts to the Lord's work (some well into eight figures), but I have learned that the smaller gifts can represent even more of a sacrifice. I know of a single mom with a couple of kids who gives in such a way that it affects deeply and costs greatly. Ultimately, the Lord decides and He rewards, but each one of us must be certain that we seek His purposes and His glory above everything else. In doing so, we are wise practitioners of the 360° stewardship of money.

How to use your things. If you love things and have an inordinate desire to have them, it can weigh you down and impede your spiritual progress. But the proper attitude toward the things of this world can have a liberating effect. Three keys have helped me keep life in balance:

1. Enjoy things, but don't cherish them. God is not opposed to our enjoying His blessings upon us. As J. B. Phillips writes, God isn't leaning over the balcony of heaven just waiting for us to enjoy something so that He can say, "Cut that out!" No, the Lord is pleased when His children find pleasure in what He has given. However, our attachment must be to Him, not to the things themselves. "Set your affections on things above, not on earthly things," says Colossians 3:2.

2. Share things joyfully, not reluctantly. It's good to share from our material possessions because in sharing we can bless others just as God has blessed us. Some dear friends of mine were once faced with a great financial need as they prepared to return to the mission field. Their plan had been to sell their car and all their household goods prior to their departure, but they felt impressed by the Lord to give away everything instead. With great joy they handed over the keys to their car to a needy couple, and to a local church they gave all their belongings to furnish a house for visiting missionaries. As an expression of love, that same church took up a surprise offering for my friends and presented them with a check that amounted to more than double what they could have received from selling their car and furnishings. God blessed them, they blessed others, and then God blessed them again! This is how sharing should be—giving of our things joyfully, not because we feel obligated or duty-bound. God loves a cheerful giver, not a reluctant one.

3. Think like a pilgrim, not a settler. The lyrics of an old gospel song say, "This world is not my home, I'm just a passin' thru. My treasures are laid up, somewhere beyond the blue." It sounds corny, but it's actually true and it is based upon the words of Jesus Himself: "Do not store up for yourselves treasures on earth, where moth and rust destroy, and where thieves break in and steal. But store up for yourselves treasures in heaven, where moth and rust do not destroy, and where thieves do not break in and steal. For where your treasure is, there your heart will be also."[2] We are indeed pilgrims, not settlers. As Paul reminded the Philippians, "our citizenship is in heaven."[3]

7 Things to Never Forget

In the 360° stewardship of every asset it is vital to think wisely. To do that, take to heart these important insights—7 things to never forget:

1. Never forget to use things and love people (not vice versa). Things have a way of capturing our interest and arresting our affections. It is amazing, in fact, how much of a pull money and material things can have upon us, making us elevate their importance completely out of reason. God's design is that we use things and love people, but what often happens is that we use people and love things! John wrote, "Do not love the world [that is, this temporal world in which we live] or the things in the world. For if anyone loves the world, the love of the Father is not in Him."[4]

Once while He was teaching the multitudes, Jesus was interrupted by a man who blurted out, "Teacher, tell my brother to divide the inheritance with me."[5] Jesus responded with words that exposed the man's true problem of greed: "Watch out! Be on your guard against all kinds of greed; a man's life does not consist in the abundance of his possessions."[6] What a powerful summation of what matters. It's not about things; it's about people. It's not about us; it's about God.

What a powerful summation of what matters. It's not about things; it's about people. It's not about us; it's about God.

2. Never forget that little things can make a big difference. I vividly recall a sermon preached by my pastor when I was just a teenager. He began his message by holding up a smooth stone, like one you would find in a streambed. "Little things can make a very big difference," he said, as he began a brilliant exposition of the story of David and Goliath.[7] The giant

Goliath, the mightiest warrior of the Philistine forces, towered to a height of "six cubits and a span." By today's measurements he stood nine feet nine inches tall—more than two feet taller than the tallest man in the NBA! Every morning and evening for 40 days the giant had blustered and threatened the army of Israel, led by King Saul. "Send out your best man to fight me," Goliath shouted. "If I win, you will be our slaves. If he wins, we will be your slaves." But there were no takers, and the level of fear in the Israelite camp was increasing. Then David showed up, sized up the situation and offered to face the massive foe. Refusing the king's armor, David went to battle Goliath armed with only a leather sling and five stones. Of course, David prevailed by slinging one of those smooth stones with absolute precision. It sailed through the air and thudded rudely into Goliath's forehead. A little thing had made a big difference.

"Little is much if God is in it." He can take the smallest gift, like the widow's mite, and multiply its effectiveness far beyond what we could ever imagine.

In the stewardship of assets it is so true that "little is much if God is in it." He can take the smallest gift, like the widow's mite, and multiply its effectiveness far beyond what we could ever imagine. Whatever the size of the resource, it can be used to honor God and accomplish His purposes.

3. Never forget that you can gain everything, but still be a big loser. It was one of the most sobering questions Jesus ever asked: "What shall it profit a man if he gain the whole world and lose his own soul?"[8] This world is full of people who have amassed great wealth and put full confidence in their riches. But every one of them will in an instant abandon all that they have accumulated; and unless they have "laid up treasure in heaven" as Jesus admonished, they will die as losers of the worst sort. Whatever you "gain" in this world has true value only to the extent that it is invested and stewarded for eternity.

4. Never forget that you can give all you have, yet invest it all as well. One of the wonderful paradoxes of the Christian life is that whatever you give away in Jesus' name produces not a loss but a profit—a spiritual profit that accrues in a heavenly account. The God-honoring steward is not one who holds on to wealth but who is willing to let go of it and give it away for that which is most important. The famous explorer and missionary David Livingstone had this attitude toward worldly resources. In his journal he wrote, "I place no value on anything I have or may possess, except in relation to the kingdom of God. If anything will advance the interests of the kingdom, it shall be given away or kept, only as by giving or keeping it I shall most promote the glory of Him to whom I owe all my hopes in time or eternity."

5. Never forget that you will give an account to God. Accountability is a subject we looked at earlier, but it's helpful to mention it once again. I try to remind myself every day to live in a way that will prepare me to stand before the Lord and give a good account of my stewardship. I want to be faithful and wise in managing all that God has entrusted to me, not because I think it will determine my eternal salvation but because it is a gift that I can give to Him who gave me life itself.

6. Never forget to be willing to give and willing to give up. I love the biographies of missionary pioneers. There is a raw beauty in their devotion to Christ and their determination to extend the frontiers of the Gospel. Many of their stories are filled with examples of the exceptional stewardship of assets. In his book, *The Living Faith*, Lloyd Douglas recounts an episode in the life of missionary Thomas Hearne: "In his journey to the mouth of the Coppermine River, Hearne wrote that a few days after they had started on their expedition, a party of Indians stole most of their supplies. His comment on the apparent misfortune was: 'The weight of our baggage being so much lightened, our next day's journey was more swift and pleasant.' Hearne was en route to something very important; and the loss of a few sides of bacon and a couple of bags of flour meant nothing more than an easing of the load. Had he been holed in somewhere, in a cabin, resolved to spend his last days eking out an existence, and living on capital previously collected, the loss of some of his stores would probably have worried him almost to death."

How we respond to "losing" some of our assets for the sake of the Lord's work depends upon whether we are on the move or waiting for our last stand.

7. Never forget that the way to multiply your trust is by trusting the Multiplier. Each one of us is given a sacred trust and we are charged with the responsibility of multiplying that trust for the Lord. This is fundamentally a matter of faith: we multiply our trust by trusting the Multiplier. God wants us to rely upon Him, to seek His favor, to pray for His blessing. Faith is foundational to effective stewardship.

Since the summer of 1992 I have made an annual hunting and fishing trip to Alaska. My mentor and partner on these mini-expeditions has been my dear friend, Dr. Jerry Prevo. Jerry is the senior pastor of Alaska's leading church, and he has had huge influence in shaping the state's cultural and political landscape. He is also an accomplished bush pilot and outdoorsman. Jerry is one of those friends whom you can count on in a crisis, who always takes your side, and who is a man's man! As a hunter he has few equals, with seven world-class Dall sheep trophies alone. We have shared some unforgettable times of fellowship in some of the most spectacular settings imaginable. In America's fabled "Last Frontier" Jerry and I have also faced some moments of great danger and high adventure. Every landing on the tundra or mountains is a nailbiter! But the most memorable of all our trips was the first one.

In America's fabled "Last Frontier" Jerry and I have faced some moments of great danger and high adventure. But the most memorable of all our trips was the first one.

Ironically, on that first trip I hadn't gone to Alaska to hunt. I was there to tour the Alaska National Wildlife Project and to be the guest speaker at my friend's church. Just to visit Alaska was the fulfillment of a life-long dream and I was captivated from the start. Jerry had invited me to stay a few days longer and go hunting with him. I eagerly accepted and we flew into a remote region of the Alaska Range, about 150 miles west of Anchorage near the Mulchatna Valley. We landed on a mountaintop for glassing with our binoculars, set up our tent, tied down the plane and began looking for animals. On our first hunting day Jerry and I spotted a good bull Caribou, put a stalk on him and decided to harvest him. It was an awesome experience for my first expedition in the Alaskan wilderness! After boning out the meat and salvaging the cape and horns, we loaded the plane, tied the horns on the wing and flew right off the top of that mountain.

On our way back we passed a mountainside where a number of black bears and a few grizzlies were feeding on berries. I had never seen anything like it. My license allowed me to hunt a black bear and we made a split-second decision to go for it. Jerry looked for a place to land and then brought the plane down into the tundra, bouncing to a rest. We deplaned, unloaded the gear and set up the tent. Then Jerry took off for Anchorage to drop off the caribou meat and pick up additional supplies. As the plane droned off into the distance I surveyed my assets: a tent, a sleeping bag, a gallon jug of water, a lantern, some waterproof matches, a box of granola bars, a hunting knife, a rifle and five bullets.

When the skies finally began to darken about 1 a.m. and he had not come back, I began to think that something very bad had happened.

The plan was for Jerry to return that night, but when the skies finally began to darken about 1 a.m. and he had not come back, I began to think that something very bad had happened. Although I was painfully tired, I couldn't sleep. Every time the sides of the tent shook in the wind I thought one of those grizzlies was coming in. I just laid there, caressing my borrowed rifle. Earlier that day Jerry and I had flown through Merrill Pass and he had shown me the remains of downed planes from years past and also some very recent ones. I couldn't help but think that my friend had crashed like so many others in the wilds of Alaska. I fought against letting my mind go there. Yet, Jerry had described the effect of rapid weather changes, planes running out of fuel because of powerful headwinds, pilot error and all sorts of other disconcerting things. Now I suspected that he, too, had fallen victim. How would I get word to someone, to anyone for that matter? How would anyone know that I had not been on that plane with him?

I didn't sleep at all the first night. Somehow on the second night I began to doze off, but awakened every few minutes at the howling of the wind. When the morning dawned I realized that I was all alone in a vast, remote area. That was before the days when GPS devices and satellite phones were commonplace, and I was literally out of touch with civilization of any kind. My only means of communication was a small signal mirror in a small emergency kit. The stark reality of my situation began to set in. I thought about my precious wife, Denise, and my kids back in Miami, holding them in my heart but frustrated with the impossible distance between us. I thought: *If I have to, I will walk through the mountains to get back to them.* I promised Denise that I would come home. Then I thought about my friend and his dear family, hoping against hope that he was still alive. As the hours passed with excruciating slowness I became more and more determined to survive, to somehow make it through this ordeal with God's help. More than ever in my life I needed to practice the 360° stewardship of every asset at hand.

On the first day, expecting Jerry to return quickly, I had eaten the entire box of granola bars. What a mistake! I began to think: I'm using too much of the lantern fuel for light. I need to conserve everything, especially food and water. Everything I had learned as a Cub Scout and Sea Scout, especially all those articles I had read in *Outdoor Life* magazine and all of the stories I had heard over the years began to come back. I knew that my main challenges would be to not panic, to conserve my bullets, to find food and water and to stay dry. On a brief hike away from the tent I made my first stalk on a black bear and shot it. I cleaned the meat as best I could and started frying it in the lantern top. That was my best idea. For five desperately long days, one day at a time, I stayed focused on survival. I read my Bible, prayed, kept my wits about me, watched for bears (especially grizzlies) and thought constantly about my family. I became convinced that no one knew where I was, nor could anyone have known that I was not aboard the plane with Jerry. He was such a good pilot that it was hard to imagine that he had gone down, but it was Jerry himself who told me the weather in Alaska is so unpredictable and potentially violent.

I made the decision to walk out on the sixth day if Jerry hadn't come back or someone else hadn't spotted me. I wrote a note to leave at the campsite in case someone happened upon it; and when I had finished writing that very difficult message, I loaded my pack and started down the mountain. All at once I heard the most beautiful sound—the distant sound of a plane engine. I tried to spot it above the trees. At first it was just a speck. I ripped open my pack and got out the binoculars. I looked again and saw a plane with unmistakable orange and tan markings—Jerry's plane!

The sight of that high-winged, humble bush plane with its big tundra tires was the sweetest thing I had ever seen! Jerry circled and made his approach. As soon as the wheels hit the ground I began to run toward the plane. When Jerry climbed out of the plane I could see that he was all right and I was so happy that he was OK. He greeted me with a big hug (and he's not a hugging type of guy), and said, "I'm so glad you're alive! I'm so glad you're OK!" I was shocked to hear those words and, of course, I wanted to know why he hadn't come back right away. He all but shouted, "I couldn't fly! I couldn't fly!" I had no idea what he was talking about. "Why?" I asked. He explained, "When the volcano erupted and the weather went down, no one was allowed to fly. In fact, I had to fly just above the river and tree tops to get here!" When I asked,

The sight of that high-winged, humble bush plane with its big tundra tires was the sweetest thing I had ever seen!

"What volcano?" Jerry was stunned. "You mean you didn't know that Mt. Spurr erupted right after I left you here?" I assured him that I had no idea about any volcanic eruption. "But there was a massive earthquake at the time the mountain blew," Jerry said. We were less than 12 miles away from the volcano but I hadn't felt a thing, and we figured out that it was because I was on tundra that had absorbed the shock like a thick, heavy carpet.

Soon we had all the gear packed and stowed and we were on our way back to Anchorage. Along they way, Jerry was unusually quiet and so was I, each of us filling in the details for the other between silent pauses. I had learned a lot about stewarding every asset—both tangible and intangible—during those five incredibly intense days. The constant challenge to wisely use everything that was available (and to find the things that weren't) had reminded me what really matters in life. A short time later I was on the long flight home to Miami, not in a pine box but in a coach seat that seemed remarkably comfortable. On that 5,000-mile journey south I counted and recounted God's blessings. He had graciously protected my friend and provided for me in the midst of an astonishing experience. I was so grateful to the Lord for enabling me to steward what I had and to appreciate everything, literally everything. My faith had increased, but beyond that I cherished my wife more, I loved my family more and I cared for my church more deeply than ever. As my faith was increasing during those days it occurred to me that my most significant asset is prayer. My long conversations with the Lord while stranded in that wilderness reminded me that the place may be desolate, but He will never leave me in desolation. I have been back to that same region of Alaska many times in the years since that pivotal week in 1992, and each time I go there I realize anew that the challenges of life can seem so overwhelming at times, but we have to put it all in proper perspective—an eternal perspective. The 360° stewardship of every asset is a temporal responsibility, but its impact and its importance are eternal.

CHAPTER
SEVEN
~ ~ ~ ~

KEEPING THE FAITH
Stewarding Every Commitment

You've undoubtedly heard of Mother Teresa. But chances are you've never heard of "Father" Thomas. Yet millions of people across the Indian subcontinent believe that his life has made an impact equal to the revered nun of Calcutta. M. A. Thomas is "Father" to over 10,000 children from the poorest of India's poor—orphaned and abandoned children that no one cared for until he rescued them from unspeakable deprivation. To each one he has given food and clothing and a roof over their heads and—above all—boundless love.

In 1960, having recently graduated from college in Madras, M. A. Thomas had only 200 rupees to his name—the equivalent of just $8—and virtually no earthly possessions. But in his heart was an inexpressibly great treasure that he was eager to share—a deep, genuine desire to help everyone that God would enable him to help. With his wife Ammini, then pregnant with their first child, M. A. was ready to set off by foot for the Indian state of Rajasthan—1,500 kilometers away. They were headed there because it was considered the most spiritually challenging and needy place in all of India. The young couple was prepared to walk an extraordinary distance to a place they had never seen, without the promise of a job or a place to stay. However, a few days before they were to begin their journey, they met a distinguished visitor from the United States, a man named Bill Bright. Dr. Bright, founder of the worldwide Christian ministry, Campus Crusade, heard M. A.'s testimony and was impressed with such remarkable commitment. He took $25 from his own pocket and gave it to M. A., with the promise that he would continue to send at least that much every month in missionary support. (Incidentally, Bill Bright kept his promise, sending monthly ministry gifts to India until his death in 2003).

M. A. was arrested, jailed, beaten and ordered by the magistrate to leave the city. After his release, he went back to the same intersection and began to preach the same message!

Using a portion of that first gift of $25, M. A. was able to purchase train tickets to Rajasthan. Though he and Ammini were ready and willing to walk, it would not be necessary, after all. But they had no idea what lay ahead. Arriving in the city of Kota on a blistering August day in 1960, M. A. went to the most prominent intersection and began to preach the Gospel. He was promptly arrested, jailed, beaten and ordered by the magistrate to leave the city. After his release, M. A. went back to the same intersection and began to preach the same message! Again, he was arrested, but his joyous attitude confounded the authorities. "Why are you here? And why won't you leave?" the judge demanded to know. M. A. Thomas replied, "I'm here to tell the Good News to everyone, and I can't leave because God sent me here to help those for whom no one cares." The judge was intrigued. "What is this 'good news' you have?" he asked. M. A. then shared Christ's message of hope and salvation. The judge was interested, but first he wanted to know why anyone would be interested in the poor. "Because Jesus loved the poor and the disadvantaged, I love them, too," he answered. In a culture where cows are valued more highly than the lives of some human beings, it was a radical thing to say. Reluctantly, the judge jailed M. A. for the night, but he rescinded the order that he leave the city.

Today, over four decades later, M. A. Thomas is the most beloved man in Kota, a city of two million people. He has never stopped preaching the Good News or daring to touch the "untouchables" of Indian society. Over the years, M. A. has dealt with countless crises and challenges; but along the way he has founded a college, trained thousands of ministers, built a hospital and numerous clinics, created a network of schools, and established nearly a hundred children's homes across the length and breadth of India. In the city of Kota is Emmanuel Children's Home, the first orphanage established by M. A. Thomas. Today it is a community of more than 1,500 boys and girls who otherwise wouldn't know the satisfaction of a good meal, the security of a safe home, or the joy of a loving embrace. But they experience all that and more because years ago one man made a commitment to live by faith, to give hope to the hopeless, and to love God unreservedly and love people unconditionally.

One life can make such an amazing difference! I look at the example of M. A. Thomas and think, *I want to make a difference like he has.* I see in him a man who has never had a lot of money, who still lives in a small apartment and who doesn't care about things. What he cares about is people. He is motivated every day to give, and that simple fact speaks volumes to me. You cannot make a difference in this life unless you're a giver. Takers—those who go through life claiming and keeping all they can—are, in the final analysis, just losers. Only givers are the truly successful, the truly effective.

A Commitment to Help

Giving help implies many things because help comes in many forms. It can take the shape of financial contribution, personal advice, physical assistance or emotional comfort, just to name a few examples. The mature Christian understands that help is the practical application of a spiritual discipline. Time after time along life's road we are called upon to be a friend to the friendless, a counselor to the confused, a peacemaker for the troubled, or a guide to the lost. Only the person who has made a spiritual commitment to be a 360° steward will make the most of those opportunities.

Be aware. To be a help giver, you have to be aware and sensitive to what others are thinking, feeling and experiencing. Insensitivity—willfully ignoring or disregarding other people—spoils a God-given privilege to show His love and demonstrate His character. God is kind, and His heart's desire is that we be kind, too. One "fruit of the Spirit"[1] is kindness—the gentle, caring attitude that motivates us to act compassionately toward others. It is an attitude we see in Jesus throughout the New Testament. He was attuned to the needs of people, and His kindness was strong and undeniable, always reaching out to oppressed and burdened souls around Him. He was God in human flesh, worthy of worship; yet He lowered Himself to be a kind, selfless servant.

Be tough. When you're giving help, don't pull punches when a situation calls for directness. Jesus spoke so directly and forcefully that many people who desperately needed His help rejected Him. "His sayings are too hard,"[2] they said. If you're reaching out to help someone (especially a friend) who is engaged in self-destructive behavior, don't make excuses for that person or make things too easy. Speak the truth in love[3], the Bible advises us. Giving help does not mean giving in.

Speak the truth in love, the Bible advises us... Giving help does not mean giving in.

Be tender. Frankly, it is often easier to be tough than to be tender. It can take a real effort to have patience and understanding with some people; but it can have a transformational effect. I was touched years ago in reading the story of Tom Anderson, who had murdered another man. Tom was visited in prison by his victim's mother, who came to him with a simple, specific message. Some time had passed since the crime, and God had comforted her heart. She went to the prison to tell Anderson that God loved him in spite of his horrendous sin and that he could find forgiveness in Jesus Christ. She then told him that her special message could be summed up in just three words: "I forgive you." They were such simple words, yet they overwhelmed him. After her visit, Tom prayed to God and begged for the forgiveness she had described and the kindness she had shown. There in that maximum-security prison, he was spiritually liberated, changed by the power of Christ. His life was radically affected because a woman who had every reason to despise him, had instead tenderly reached out to give help.

Be intentional. To be intentional is to take the initiative, to intercede with help even when you sense it may not be welcome. One of the greatest regrets of my life was a failure to stay connected with my brother-in-law, Dean. He had always been

> *To be intentional is to take the initiative, to intercede with help even when you sense it may not be welcome.*

the sort of guy whose smile could light up a room, with a voice that could be heard above all others, and a personality without limits. But Dean had a troubled soul, haunted with who knows what kind of torment. I wish I had been more aware of the pain he was experiencing, but I was so busy ministering to people that I missed the person—and he was right in my own family.

One night a few years ago, Dean lost all hope and gave up on his ability to sustain his life. He made his family a great dinner, left a personal note for each loved one, then went to his office and took his own life. I was on the road when I got the call from my wife. I can still hear her crying, and I can still feel the convulsed emotions. It has left a hole in our souls. Apparently we had not been sufficiently aware of his struggles, nor intentional enough in reaching out to give help to Dean when he really needed it. He may have rejected us, but that's the risk that comes with a commitment to help.

Our family is comforted by the fact that Dean had openly expressed his faith in Christ. We will see him again in heaven one day. But the loss of Dean has made me resolve to never again close my eyes or cover my ears to the need of someone I am in a position to help. It's as if God is saying to me, *Kirk, whatever someone needs, even if you have to take them on your back and carry them, that's what it means to give help.*

As Christians we are compelled to help others, not out of guilt but out of compassion. Our English word *compassion* is derived from two Latin words which literally mean, "to suffer with." To have compassion is "to suffer with" other people—to put yourself in their shoes, to feel what they feel, to endure what they endure. This is what Jesus did constantly. So great was His love and concern that He was often "moved with compassion."[4] Throughout His earthly ministry He unceasingly gave help and healing to the poor, the diseased and the needy.

God is pleased when we do what Jesus did, giving compassionate help to those who are less fortunate. James 1:27 says that "Religion that God our Father accepts as pure and faultless is this: to look after orphans and widows in their distress." Giving to those who can give nothing back is a spiritually beautiful thing, and it honors God. In Acts 10, in the story of the Roman centurion Cornelius, the Bible says that "he gave generously to those in need and prayed to God regularly." In a vision from God, an angel told him, "Your prayers and gifts to the poor have come up as a memorial offering before God."[5] As a Christian, when you give help to and for others, it is the same as giving directly to God.

We must not look the other way when opportunities come. As Christ's followers we cannot insist upon clean hands and safe risks when our world is such an ugly and unlovely place for so many suffering people.

At a restaurant recently our waitress was an impressive young lady named Emily—impressive because her face seemed to glow and her personality was so memorable. My wife and I struck up a conversation with Emily and learned that she waited on tables to make a living. But her life—her *mission*, she said—is to care for the "ladies of the night" in inner city Atlanta. She said, "when I leave here, I'm going to a neighborhood where 13-year-old girls literally sell themselves. I offer help and food and compassion in the name of Jesus." In meeting Emily I was reminded that many of us need to stop praying for opportunities and take the ones that are already there. Let's get our hands dirty, let's get out of our comfort zones, and—in the cause of Christ—let's show that we care. Whether it's an elderly person in grave need, a dying AIDS patient, a widow with little in earthly goods, or someone else in some other circumstance, what matters is that we act decisively in Jesus' name. When we give others help, we give Him honor.

A Commitment to Give

Giving is at the heart of the Christian life, at the heart of the Gospel, and at the heart of God. "For God so loved the world that he gave his one and only son..."[6] God is the infinite and perfect Giver: giving is integral to who He is. And because giving is inherent in God's character, when we give we identify with Him and we reflect His likeness.

Everything of true value is given by God. He has given us life itself—physical life in the blood that courses through our human bodies and spiritual life in the blood of His Son, Jesus Christ, whose once-for-all sacrifice makes possible our eternal salvation. God has set the pattern for giving, and there is no worthier goal than to give like He gives. But is that possible? Yes, it is not only possible; it is imperative.

As I've explored the Bible to find out what it means to be a faithful giver, I have been reminded repeatedly that giving has to do with much more than money. However, it absolutely, positively *does* have to do with money. Let's be clear about that, and make no apologies for that fact. I realize that many Christian leaders consider the giving of tithes to be an "old school" method. But when I look at the Scriptures, it is clear to me that responsible, regular giving is foundational. It is the cornerstone on which sacrificial giving is built. Responsibility and sacrifice are, in fact, common to the practice of believers in both the Old Testament and New Testament eras.

Responsibility and sacrifice are, in fact, common to the practice of believers in both the Old Testament and New Testament eras.

As a pastor I initially found it uncomfortable to teach or preach on the subject of financial giving because I had not yet reached a point of personal conviction and commitment. I had seen giving as a Christian value, similar to the importance of being a good husband, a good father, a hard worker, a dedicated witness for Christ. But I soon realized that being a giver includes both responsibility and sacrifice. I had to ask myself as a leader:

Am I a responsible giver? Am I giving regularly, consistently and faithfully—before any question of sacrificial giving is considered? I concluded that you can't give sacrificially unless you're first giving responsibly, and to me that clearly meant the tithe. I have never seen an effective argument against the biblical mandate for tithing. The Bible says, "If a man does not provide for his own house, he is worse than an infidel."[7] And what about God's house? Haggai said, "Is it a time to be living in your paneled houses while the Lord's house remains a ruin?"[8] I was ultimately able to say as a leader of my church and my home that giving—responsibly as well as sacrificially—is what God desires of us as stewards. We must be found faithful!

Our money, indeed all of our resources, don't really belong to us. They have been entrusted to us by God to manage for His purposes.

Our money, indeed all of our resources, don't really belong to us. They have been entrusted to us by God to manage for His purposes. This is not simply an opinion I have; it is a categorical expression of the Scriptures: "The earth is the Lord's, and everything in it."[9] The obedient Christian lives by a creed of stewardship, not ownership.

There is a great paradox here: I have the privilege of giving, and I get the benefit and blessing of giving; but what I am giving is not actually mine—it belongs to God. Accepting that paradox liberates me from the bondage of trying to accumulate as much as I can in life or striving constantly to have bigger and better things than my neighbors.

Giving faithfully. Faithful givers are faithful stewards. In fact, the first and most important attribute of a steward is faithfulness. The Bible says emphatically: "It is required that those who have been given a trust must prove faithful."[10] The "trust" encompasses all the material resources given to us by God. His plan is that we manage those assets in a way that is spiritually wise and profitable.

There is a two-fold significance to giving faithfully. First, it means giving by faith in God, mindful that He is Lord of all. Second, it means giving in a faithful, dependable manner. In both meanings, God provides the power and we follow through with the practice. He puts faith in our hearts and we exercise that faith by giving for His glory to accomplish His purposes.

My years as a pastor convinced me that one who gives money faithfully is much more likely to faithfully give time and ability and other resources. Money is a major determinant of life, for as Jesus said, "Where your treasure is, there your heart will be also."[11] I've counseled with many people whose struggles and crises can be traced directly to their "treasure"—and consequently, their heart—being in the wrong place. Faithfulness in giving—to the right purposes, in the right way—has a powerfully positive effect and keeps our priorities in order.

Giving gracefully. The Apostle Paul asks a monumental question: "He who did not spare his own Son, but gave him up for us all—how will he not also, along with him, graciously give us all things?"[12] Everything we have—everything—is a gift of God. I can think of anything in my life, small or large, no matter what it is, and tell you absolutely that I didn't earn it or deserve it. The house I live in, the car I drive, the clothes I wear, the money in my bank account—whatever it is, without exception, I have because God graciously gave it to me. In His infinite love, He smiled on me and blessed me—just as He loves and blesses you.

So, when it comes down to how I am going to give, I must look first to the example of God. I see that He gives graciously, and I know that I am to give graciously, too. This means that I must never give in a way that magnifies my own magnanimity. Have you ever had someone give you a gift and then constantly remind you what a great gift they gave? Graceful giving never draws attention to itself, but directs attention to God. Graceful giving seeks to glorify God, not to better one's own bottom line. And graceful giving is driven by a desire to lift up the recipient, not lift up the giver.

Giving proportionally. A powerful principle of stewardship is that God's provision dictates the believer's proportion. In other words, what He provides determines what we give. If He gives a little, from that little we are to give; if He gives abundantly, from that abundance we are to give. The measure of His giving determines the measure of our giving. As Jesus said, "To whom much is given, much is required."[13]

Don't worry about how much you have or don't have to give. Instead, give in proportion to everything you have received. My personal conviction is that giving begins with the tithe and extends beyond that to offerings for the Lord's work. The tithe is the simplest proportion to understand: it is 10% of the total. For me, it's easy to know what constitutes my tithe to the Lord's work: What does my W-2 say at the end of the year? What is one-tenth of that? Giving that amount over the years has never had anything but a positive effect in my life. But the tenth is really just the baseline. Giving above and beyond that level moves the giver into exceptional or even sacrificial giving.

Relying upon the Lord and depending upon Him as our source, we grow in grace as we give. In the process, giving becomes a spiritually enlivening experience, for as we die to self we come alive in faith.

The young churches of Macedonia were persecuted severely and were materially poor, but in spite of their poverty they excelled in giving.

Giving sacrificially. In the first century after Christ, the young churches of Macedonia were persecuted severely and were materially poor, but in spite of their poverty they excelled in giving. Specifically, they gave to a ministry project that the apostle Paul had initiated; and they gave in a most remarkable way: sacrificially, beyond their ability, willingly and eagerly—of themselves to God and of their resources to God's work. Here's how the Bible describes the giving Christians of Macedonia: "Brothers, we want you to know about the grace that God has given the Macedonian churches. Out of the most severe trial, their overflowing joy and their extreme poverty welled up in rich generosity. For I testify that they gave as much as they were able, and even beyond their ability. Entirely on their own, they urgently pleaded with us for the privilege of sharing in this service to the saints. And they did not do as we expected, but they gave themselves first to the Lord and then to us in keeping with God's will."[14]

Study the great causes described in the Bible—like the cause to which the Macedonians gave, or the building projects for the Tabernacle and the Temple—and you'll see right away that they were funded through gifts above and beyond the tithe. Exceptional needs require exceptional giving—giving beyond the baseline, giving that is bold and generous and sacrificial.

Giving globally. The cause of Christ is an all-encompassing cause touching every person in every place—to "the ends of the earth."[15] "For God so loved the world..."[16] The world of people, that is—every person of every era throughout history. "For God so loved the world that he gave..." God's love motivated Him to give, offering His own Son as our substitute and savior.

God loves and God gives globally, and this is our inspiration.

God loves and God gives globally, and this is our inspiration. Faithful Christians give globally, earnestly supporting the worldwide work of Christ. In fact, the most spiritually vibrant believers I know are those who have a passion for world missions and who back up that passion with generous gifts to the Lord's work.

When Jesus sent out His disciples to declare the Gospel, He told them, "Freely you have received, freely give."[17] And that's what they did, freely giving all that they could in His name. Today, 20 centuries later, that is still the priority for us as followers of Christ—to faithfully, gracefully, proportionally and sacrificially sow the seeds of His truth throughout the world, knowing we will reap an eternal harvest.

A Commitment to Witness

Bono. His name instantly conjures images of a larger-than-life personality, the brightest light in a constellation of rock stars. But Bono, lead vocalist for U2 and unabashed activist, is surprisingly different from the flashy image. Behind his ever-present sunglasses are eyes that see the world clearly and a mind that grasps spiritual realities. In the compelling book, *Bono: In Conversation With Michka Assayas*, he was asked about his faith. Bono said, "I'd be in big trouble if Karma was going to finally be my judge. It doesn't excuse my mistakes, but I'm holding out for Grace. I'm holding out that Jesus took my sins onto the Cross, because I know who I am, and I hope I don't have to depend on my own religiosity."

Assayas replied, "The Son of God who takes away the sins of the world. I wish I could believe in that." To which Bono answered, "...The point of the death of Christ is that Christ took on the sins of the world, so that what we put out did not come back to us, and that our sinful nature does not reap the obvious death. It's not our own good works that get us through the gates of Heaven."[18]

The journalist, true to his profession, was trying to get something out of Bono—a bold statement, a shocking admission or a juicy comment. What he was given was perhaps bolder and more shocking than he had anticipated. A world-famous musician had just given him the Gospel. Who would ever expect that? Who would ever think that a man who personifies hipness would talk so seamlessly about grace, about atonement, about the deity of Jesus Christ? But he did, because he was ready to share passionately the truth that sets humans free.

Bono was practicing an ancient principle. It was expressed this way in 63 A.D.: "In your hearts set apart Christ as Lord. Always be prepared to give an answer to everyone who asks you to give the reason for the hope that you have."[19] Bono was prepared to give the reason for his hope in Christ, and that's precisely what he did. Had he given the journalist a million dollars (which he could easily do), it would have been worth nothing in comparison to the truth he communicated.

A lot of people have a hard time believing that there is truth to be found. Many are burned by bad experiences or let down by life in some way, and they're left with scars and suspicions. Others are turned off by the very idea of absolute truth. They just can't see how one truth would be exclusive and transcendent above all the rest. It just doesn't seem to show "tolerance."

A friend of mine was passing through a train station when a bit of graffiti caught his eye. An evangelistic vandal had scrawled,

Christ is the answer.

Underneath those words, in a different script, a second tagger had written,

What's the question?

Beneath that, a third philosopher had added a final commentary,

Life is the question.

Three people, less than a dozen words, but a profound "discussion" about a subject that touches every human being. If Christ is the answer—the answer to life itself—then there's no getting around the implications. If I don't connect with Him in some definitive way, how can I hope to experience life in the fullest sense? If I'm to believe C. S. Lewis, Jesus made some claims that are either outrageously wrong or categorically right. Lewis, of course, goes with the latter. And so do I.

When I look at what Jesus actually said, though He spoke the words twenty centuries ago, I get goosebumps of amazement. In the days just before His passion, Jesus was meeting with a group of His followers, encouraging them to look hopefully to the future. "Do not let your hearts be troubled," He told them, "...You know the way to the place where I am going." Thomas—the infamously "doubting" Thomas—blurted out, "Lord, we don't know where you are going, so how can we know the way?" And in the most categorical, leave-no-doubts manner, Jesus replied, "I am the way and the truth and the life. No one comes to the Father except through me."[20] Yes, He was saying to Thomas and the others, Yes, you do know the way because you know *me*.

- - -

When I look at what Jesus actually said, though He spoke the words twenty centuries ago, I get goosebumps of amazement.

- - -

When Jesus was brought before the Roman governor Pontius Pilate, He told him, "You are right in saying I am a king. In fact, for this reason I was born, and for this I came into the world, to testify to the truth. Everyone on the side of truth listens to me." Pilate, either thoroughly confused or profoundly convicted replied, "What is truth?"[21]

Everyone on the side of truth listens to me. Wow, what a statement! That's as categorical and straightforward as you can get. But Jesus said it, and we have to deal with it. There is no room for compromise or halfway positions: what He said places every human being on one side or the other. That's why He boldly said, "He who is not with me is against me."[22]

The biblical record tells us explicitly that truth is wrapped up in a Person—in who Jesus was, what He said and what He did. Look at any calendar and you'll see that His life is the dividing line in history. It is also the dividing line in every human heart. To find Him is to find the way, to know Him is to know the truth, to have Him is to have life itself. The Gospel—literally, the Good News—is the message of His redeeming, sacrificial love. In receiving and believing that message, trusting only in Him, a person receives the "gift of God"[23]—eternal life.

> *Look at any calendar and you'll see that His life is the dividing line in history. It is also the dividing line in every human heart.*

Whenever I meet a famous person—and I've had the opportunity to meet several—I find myself talking about that person, whoever it is, for several days afterwards. Perhaps you've had that same experience. It's as if some kind of energy has been transmitted and you keep thinking about that person and you're keenly aware of their fame, fortune or importance. You don't have to work up the courage to mention your "connection" with whomever the person is. You simply talk openly and eagerly.

When I think about the fact that, spiritually speaking, I personally know the most important figure in all of history, it makes me shake my head in astonishment. It also makes me realize that I should talk naturally and freely about my relationship to Jesus Christ—as freely as I would talk if I had just met the President of the United States. The difference is that I may not be in a position to introduce anyone to the President, but I am in a position to introduce another person to Jesus Christ.

In stewarding the commitment to witness we are stewarding the truth about Christ. When I communicate to someone His story, His message and His relevance, I am communicating truth. It isn't truth because I said it is, but because He said so. "I am the truth," He declared. So, for the follower of Christ, the pressing question is: How can I clearly and most effectively communicate truth by giving Christ to another person? Or, to put it another way, How can I give the reason for my hope?

The simplest advice I can give is this: If you have believed in Jesus Christ alone, if you have received God's gift of eternal life through Him, then determine to get to know Him in a spiritually intimate way. Think about Him. Communicate with Him day to day, even moment to moment, in prayer. Read His words, meditating on them and memorizing them, not out of ritual, but out of love.

Years ago when I first met my wife, Denise, whenever we were apart and I would get a letter from her, I would cherish it to the point that I would know the words by heart, even though I never consciously attempted to memorize them. That's the way it is with love. If you're in love, you value every communication with your loved one, you prize that person's words, and your intimacy deepens because of it.

It's become easier and easier for me to talk about my faith in Jesus Christ. I've learned to not think of it as some kind of religious duty to perform or obligation to fulfill. Christ has transformed my life and given me purpose. So, to talk about Him is simply a matter of communicating the significance of that transformation. He's the reason for my hope and the source of my freedom. He is truth, and that truth has set me free.

After the historic Emancipation Proclamation of 1863, Abraham Lincoln was meeting with a group of newly-freed slaves when one of the men knelt at Lincoln's feet to thank him. The President reached down, took the man's hand and brought him to his feet. "Please don't bow to me," said Lincoln, "I'm a man just like you, and we both should bow only to the One who created us and truly gives us our freedom." Old Abe had a keen understanding of truth. He could look into the face of a former slave and know that in God's eyes they were no different, that they were both in need of the freedom that only God can give.

Has the truth set you free? Then talk about it. Give that truth to the people you meet on life's pathway. Let them know the reason for your hope!

A Commitment to Love

If the Bible were a door, what would be its hinges?

Believe it or not, Jesus answered this question when he was asked, "Teacher, which is the greatest commandment in the Law?" The man who posed the question was a lawyer whose intention was to entrap Jesus, provoking Him to say something the Pharisees could hold against Him. But, being infinitely wiser than his inquisitors, Jesus replied: "'Love the Lord your God with all your heart and with all your soul and with all your mind.' This is the first and greatest commandment." But He did not stop there. Jesus continued, "And the second is like it: 'Love your neighbor as yourself.'" And to top it off, He then made a remarkable summary statement: "All the Law and the Prophets hang on these two commandments."[24]

If you love the Lord your God completely and you love your neighbor sincerely, you are living by the essence of all biblical teaching.

Jesus was saying categorically that the entire Old Testament hangs on the hinges of these two commandments. If you love the Lord your God completely and you love your neighbor sincerely, you are living by the essence of all biblical teaching. Amazing.

The Bible is clear in telling us that love is the greatest. It is the greatest quality. It is the greatest virtue. It is the greatest gift.

Nothing tops love. It is greater than eloquence, greater than knowledge, greater than faith, greater than sacrifice, greater than hope, greater than anything.

"If I speak in the tongues of men and of angels, but have not love, I am only a resounding gong or a clanging cymbal. If I have the gift of prophecy and can fathom all mysteries and all knowledge, and if I have a faith that can move mountains, but have not love, I am nothing. If I give all I possess to the poor and surrender my body to the flames, but have not love, I gain nothing... And now these three remain: faith, hope and love. But the greatest of these is love." [25]

Days before the traumatic events of His passion, Jesus said to His followers, "A new command I give you: Love one another. As I have loved you, so you must love one another. By this all men will know that you are my disciples, if you love one another." [26] Imagine what must have gone through their minds when days later they thought about one phrase in particular: "As I have loved you..." No one had ever loved them as Jesus had loved—selflessly, completely, sacrificially. And that's how they were to love one another!

A powerful proof that we are truly followers of Christ is the love we demonstrate for other Christians. Philosopher and theologian Francis Schaeffer said that this one thing—genuine love—is the true mark of the Christian, transcending everything else.

The evidence of a spiritually empowered life is described in a list of nine qualities in Galatians 5:22-23. "The fruit of the Spirit," it says, "is love, joy, peace, patience, kindness, goodness, faithfulness, gentleness and self-control." Leading the list is love, and many biblical scholars believe that love by itself is *the* "fruit of the Spirit" and all the other qualities are simply by-products of love. Looking at the Scriptures, it's hard to disagree with that conclusion. There is no joy without love, no peace without love, no patience without love, no other virtue without love.

What does love look like? The highest and best description is found in 1 Corinthians, chapter 13, a memorable, moving passage of Scripture that reads with poetic beauty.

> "Love is patient, love is kind. It does not envy, it does not boast, it is not proud. It is not rude, it is not self-seeking, it is not easily angered, it keeps no record of wrongs. Love does not delight in evil but rejoices with the truth. It always protects, always trusts, always hopes, always perseveres. Love never fails. But where there are prophecies, they will cease; where there are tongues, they will be stilled; where there is knowledge, it will pass away. For we know in part and we prophesy in part, but when perfection comes, the imperfect disappears... Now we see but a poor reflection as in a mirror; then we shall see face to face. Now I know in part; then I shall know fully, even as I am fully known. And now these three remain: faith, hope and love. But the greatest of these is love." [27]

Love is patient. It enables us to endure difficult people and troubling situations with a longsuffering spirit.

Love is kind. It prompts us, even when we are treated unkindly, to respond with the kindness and gentleness of Jesus.

Love does not envy. When we look at others who have more "success" or more of this world's wealth, love guards the heart, stifling the urge to envy. It makes us content with what we have rather than dissatisfied with what we don't have.

Love does not boast. Since everything we have and everything we are is a gift of God's grace, love makes us realize that there is no sensible reason to brag about ourselves.

Love guards the heart, stifling the urge to envy. It makes us content with what we have rather than dissatisfied with what we don't have.

Love is not proud. Pride—self-absorption and complete disregard for God—is one of the ugliest of all human tendencies. It is the diametric opposite of love.

Love is not rude. It doesn't interfere, insult or step on others' feelings.

Love is not self-seeking. In an age of utter self-centeredness, it stands against the tide, putting concern for others ahead of one's own interests.

Love is not easily angered. It doesn't fly off the handle at the slightest discomfort or offense.

Love keeps no record of wrongs. It has no "little black book" hidden in the heart, archiving the faults, failings and sins of others.

Love does not delight in evil. It finds no joy or satisfaction in unwholesome behavior or Christless attitudes.

Love rejoices with the truth. It is genuinely pleased when truth prevails, when right is done.

Love always protects. Like a mother guarding her young child, love guards what is precious. It protects against unfair personal attacks, hurtful gossip about other people, or anything that is counter to what is right and just.

Love always trusts. It believes the best to the nth degree.

Love always hopes. It looks positively to the future even where there seems no logical reason for confidence or certainty.

Love always perseveres. It gives, but never gives up. It holds on, no matter what storms may threaten. In a friendship, it endures difficulties and disagreements. In a marriage, it hangs on in spite of differences that others would deem irreconcilable. In the experiences of life, it never loses its grip.

Love never fails. It ultimately wins out. It reaches the finish line regardless of pitfalls and obstacles along the path.

Love is the ultimate quality of the person who practices 360° stewardship—the motivating power that drives us to do the right thing, say the right word, show the right attitude. Think back to the vignettes of people in this chapter...

What motivated M. A. Thomas to put up with beatings, imprisonments, ridicule, persecution and harassment for the sake of Christ?

What motivated the believers of Macedonia to give generously in spite of their own poverty?

What motivated Bono to share his faith in Christ?

In every case, there is one underlying motivation: True, Christlike love. On all the gifts we give, this is the "wrapping paper"—the beautiful covering for everything we offer to God and to one another.

I encourage you: faithfully steward every commitment. Give help to those who need your compassion and assistance. Give your money and resources, wisely investing to reap a spiritual return. Give the gift of Truth to those who ask you the reason for your hope in Christ. And, above all, give the gift of Love, the gift that transcends all others in value and importance.

May God give you wisdom and strength in the 360° stewardship of your life.

REFERENCES

Introduction

1   1 Timothy 6:11-14

2   1 Kings 3:12

3   1 Timothy 6:17-19

Chapter 1

1   Genesis 1:14

2   Psalm 90:4

3   Lewis, C. S., *The Screwtape Letters*, Letter XV, pp. 67-68

4   Lewis, C. S., *Miracles*, Appendix B, pp. 176-177

5   Philippians 3:20

6   Psalm 90:12

7   Philippians 2:5-11

8   Philippians 2:12-13

9   Philippians 2:14-15

10 Philippians 2:16

11 John 20:21 (NKJV)

12 James 4:13-14a

13 James 4:14b-17

14 1 Corinthians 10:31

15 Psalm 118:24

16 See Luke 13:10-17

17 Luke 13:12

18 Luke 13:14

19 Luke 13:15-16

20 Luke 13:17

Chapter 2

1   Ephesians 5:15-17

2   1 Corinthians 16:8-9

3   Philippians 3:12-14

4   Judges 4:6-7

5   Judges 4:8

6   Judges 4:9-10

7   Judges 4:14

8   Judges 4:14

9   Judges 4:15-16

10 Judges 4:17

11 Judges 4:18

12 Judges 4:19-20

13 Judges 4:21

14 Judges 4:22

15 Judges 4:23

16 Judges 5:24

17 Judges 5:31a

18 Judges 5:31b

19 Acts 1:8

20 Matthew 28:18-20

21 1 Peter 3:15

22 See Luke 10:25-37

23 Ephesians 5:15-17

24 Ephesians 6:13-18

Chapter 3

1 Genesis 1:1

2 Colossians 1:16-17

3 Genesis 1:26

4 See Matthew 3:16-17; Mark 1:9-11; Luke 3:21-22; John 1:29-34

5 See John 3:16 (KJV)

6 Acts 4:12

7 John 14:6

8 See Matthew 4:19; Mark 1:17

9 See Matthew 28:19

10 John 15:8

11 Colossians 3:16

12 Acts 20:27

13 John 1:40-42

14 John 9:25

15 Philippians 4:8

16 1 Corinthians 11:1

17 Philippians 1:3

18 See Philippians 1:4-8

19 See Philippians 1:5

20 Matthew 25:21

21 Hebrews 13:17

22 Romans 13:8

Chapter 4

1 Matthew 6:9-13

2 Matthew 7:7-8

3 Matthew 7:9-11

4 1 John 1:9

5 2 Corinthians 10:3-4

6 James 5:16b

7 James 5:16a

8 John 17:3

9 John 17:11

10 John 17:15

11 John 17:13

12 John 17:17

13 John 17:20

14 John 17:23

15 Ephesians 4:3

Chapter 5

1 Exodus 4:1-5

2 Acts 17:6 (KJV)

3 James 1:17

4 James 1:18

5 Acts 3:6-8

6 Acts 4:12

7 Acts 4:14

8 Acts 4:19

9 Acts 4:20

10 Ephesians 1:11

11 Colossians 1:27

12 1 Corinthians 4:1-2

Chapter 6

1 See Luke 12:48b (KJV)

2 Matthew 6:19-21

3 Philippians 3:20

4 1 John 2:15 (NKJV)

5 Luke 12:13

6 Luke 12:15

7 See 1 Samuel 17:1-54

8 Luke 9:25 (KJV)

Chapter 7

1 Galatians 5:22

2 John 6:60

3 Ephesians 4:15

4 Matthew 9:36 (KJV)

5 Acts 10:2-4

6 John 3:16

7 1 Timothy 5:8

8 Haggai 1:4

9 Psalm 24:1

10 1 Corinthians 4:2

11 Matthew 6:21

12 Romans 8:32

13 Luke 12:48 (KJV)

14 2 Corinthians 8:1-5

15 Acts 1:8

16 John 3:16

17 Matthew 10:8

18 Assayas, Michka. *Bono: In Conversation with Michka Assayas.* New York: Riverhead Press, 2005, page 205.

19 1 Peter 3:15

20 John 14:1-6

21 John 18:37-38

22 Matthew 12:30

23 Romans 6:23

24 Matthew 22:36-39

25 1 Corinthians 13:1-3, 13

26 John 13:34

27 1 Corinthians 13:4-13